I Will Save You
To Make You A Blessing

By

Greg Budd

Printed by
Remnant Publications
Coldwater, MI

I Will Save You to Make You a Blessing

Cover Illustration by Wanda Wincek
© Wanda Wincek

Cover Design by Penny Hall

Edited by Jeannie Bachholz

This edition published 2004

Copyright © 2003 by
Greg Budd

Printed in the United States of America
All Rights Reserved

ISBN 0-9748471-0-0

Acknowledgments

I would like to thank my wife, Lesa, for urging me to make the stories of my life a book. I am thankful for her faithful support as we shared many of these experiences together. I am so thankful to be blessed with such an inspirational partner in a shared ministry for the Lord.

I would like to thank our special friends, Dan and Karen Houghton, for their support and encouragement in the writing of this book.

I would also like to thank our friends, Chas and Tami Lewis, for their insights and support.

I would like to give special recognition to our friends, Dennis and Miline Linder, for their important contribution.

It would be impossible for me to express the impact of the Christianity modeled and the inspiration I have gained on my spiritual journey from my pastor-friend, Peter Neri. I am so thankful for one that will allow God to see the lost through his eyes, touch the hurting through his hands, and allow his lips to be anointed with the grace from above as he positions himself unreservedly in the service of his Savior as an intercessor and a warrior.

I would like to express my thanks and gratitude to Wanda Wincek for using her talent and intimate walk with her friend Jesus to be used as a vessel of inspiration and expression as she painted the picture used to illustrate the front cover.

Dedication

I would like to dedicate this book to the special people in my life that knew what it meant to wrestle with God for the salvation of a lost loved one in the face of the most hopeless and discouraging evidences.

To my father and mother, Joe and Patsy Budd, who personally modeled the loving power of the gospel in their lives as well as an undaunted faith in prevailing prayer that "availeth much" in the spiritual battlefield. I am thankful not only for their powerful prayers of the past but for their continued intercession for Lesa and myself as we share the gospel in churches, schools and prisons.

To my sister, Sherry Budd, who has also modeled an intimate walk with her God as well as joining the army of intercessors that wrestled with God as did Jacob when he refused to let go of the arm of God without a blessing. It would be impossible to enumerate the many creative ways that she has used to express her love as "Aunt Sherry," winning the hearts of our children right from the very beginning.

In loving memory of my grandmother, Josephine Budd, who would pray all night for me when she felt a compelling sense of urgency.

To the many other family members who joined in the battle for my soul.

I also include in this Key Persons List the loving church family of my childhood and youth in Moses Lake, Washington, who modeled the power of a corporate family interpreting its roll as a redemptive body for the cause of Christ.

Contents

Forward 6
1. Thin Ice 9
2. With Peter in Pilate's Courtyard 15
3. The Death Angel Passes By 21
4. Returning to My Father's House 30
5. Weeping May Tarry for a Night, but Joy Cometh in the Morning 36
6. Troubled By Spirits of Darkness 40
7. Lord, If We Could Choose 50
8. Our New Home 57
9. Concrete Trouble 63
10. Sharing the Gospel 71
11. Life-Saving Mosquitoes 79
12. Fiery Darts of the Devil 85
13. A Valiant Evangelist 92
14. Our God is Faithful 105
15. Praising God in the Storm 110
16. Hurricane Mitch 117
17. Our God is a Very Present Help in Time of Need 123
18. Conclusion 132

Forward

This book is excellent! It is easy to read and is one of those books that is hard to put down once you start reading. (I suggest you start the book early in the evening.) In fact, the stories are so captivating, I sat my family down (including two teenage boys) and read some of the chapters to them. It held their attention, too! That is because chapter after chapter contains stories about real life situations and struggles that Greg personally faced and how Jesus guided him through them, or taught him lessons by them, or just plain saved his life in spite of them. What makes these stories of his life even more interesting is the fact that we can readily identify with them. It is uncanny how I found myself reading and thinking that this is a story about me, not Greg! When you add Greg's transparency and honesty it makes it possible for all of us to learn valuable lessons that will grow our faith.

Also, the Jesus Greg reveals throughout his book is one that you will love to know and worship. Perhaps you, dear reader, are looking for a Savior who is real to you, a Savior you can identify with. You will find Him within these pages! How do I know? At the beginning of this volume, Greg relates experiences in which we clearly witness the struggle for his soul between Jesus and Satan. And yet, though Greg often surrenders to the wrong side, we vividly recognize Jesus' persistence in persuing him! Towards the middle of this manuscript, Jesus' persistence finally wears Greg down until he ultimately surrenders, and a drastic change takes place in his life. And though all his problems do not end, he carries through the end of his book a Peace and a Presence in every situation he faces. What is the end result? You, dear reader, as you pour over this volume, cannot help but recognize that same loving, persistent Savior is there for you. Through the pages of this book you will hear Him calling to you. For "Jesus Christ is the same yesterday, and today and forever," and "God is no respecter of persons" (Hebrews 13:8, Acts 10:34).

Finally, I want you to know that my prayer for you is that this precious, blessed book brings to you an unshakable confidence in the same friend that Greg has found and wants you to know. That friend is Jesus. And should you choose to be worn down as Greg was, you too, will find the Peace and Presence that "will never leave you nor forsake you" (Hebrews 13:5). God bless you!

Pastor Peter Neri

1
Thin Ice

It was one of those frosty, sparkling December mornings; one that a photographer might choose to illustrate a winter month on a calendar. Outside, the trees looked as though shimmering glass crystals decorated every branch and limb. Early morning sunlight shone through the frosty panes of our little classroom, adding to the winter wonderland. How would I ever be able to wait for school to come to an end? For an eighth-grade boy who loved winter fun, a newly frozen lake was waiting for his skates to become the first of the season to carve initials in that giant sheet of frozen glass.

Our little school was only about three or four minutes walk from the edge of a small lagoon that quickly froze over, becoming our playground for recess and after-school hours during the winter months. Teachers and parents joined in the search for ice skates to ensure that each student would have an opportunity to join in the fun. As you might imagine, ice skating became an event eagerly anticipated each winter. To add to this young boy's excitement, our family lived only a few miles away from the little playground lagoon on a rather remote portion of Moses Lake in the state of Washington. Every year there were church socials and parties with bonfires and hot drinks on the ice at the lakefront down below our house.

This afternoon would be the long-awaited moment to try out the newly frozen ice. Throughout the long hours of what seemed like a never-ending school day, fanciful pictures of gliding across the newly frozen lake danced in my mind. Finally, the bell rang and we were on our way home. Perhaps you can remember a time

I Will Save You to Make You a Blessing

when it seemed to take hours to travel a few miles. This was one of those days. Arriving home from school, I dashed through the door and ran to change into warm winter clothes. With my skates in hand, I sprinted down the long hill to the lake, eager to begin the fun.

The ice was just as I had imagined it: one giant sheet of glass reflecting the sun's late afternoon colors and shadows. I quickly laced my skates and with two quick tugs my gloves were on. I was ready for the first adventure of the season. I stepped carefully out onto the ice to test it with my body weight. Each year, the fire department issued a statement specifying the necessary thickness and precautions for safe ice. I looked carefully at the cloudy layer of tiny bubbles suspended above the dark water beneath. It certainly looked like the necessary four inches necessary for safe ice. I made several passes parallel to the shore, making sure the ice would safely support my weight as I was the first pioneer to carve his mark on the newly frozen lake.

Without even a tiny ripple to mar the surface of this newly frozen sheet of glass, it felt more like I was flying than skating. I couldn't wait for the church socials and parties that would soon take place in this very spot. Then my eye caught sight of the island just a quarter mile or so from shore. Every year we skated out to this little island as part of our ice skating adventure. With the youthful, adventuresome spirit of an eighth grader, the thought of being the first one to skate to the island became an irresistible call. Only for a fleeting moment did thoughts of precaution pass through my mind as I set my course for the island.

I quickly picked up speed and within minutes had crossed half the distance to the island. Suddenly, without any sort of warning, the ice made a loud crack and then gave way beneath me. With a giant splash, I dropped into the dark waters below. Instinctively, my arms shot out catching bits of fragmented ice that kept my head and neck suspended above the slushy ice water. Instantly, the heavy, insulated clothing I was wearing filled with water, causing me to feel like giant sandbags were tied around my body. The added weight created the sensation of some unseen force attempting to draw me beneath the surface of the water. The ice skates I was wearing created additional problems, providing just the opposite effect that flippers would to a swimmer in the summer.

As I frantically attempted to tread water, the frigid temperature

Thin Ice

created by the ice caused a feeling of numbness to rapidly spread from limb to limb, paralyzing every muscle in my body. Breathing instantly became a series of rapid, shallow gasps that felt as if some giant force were squeezing my lungs, causing me to struggle violently for air. I knew I must try to somehow climb out of this dark, icy hole if it wasn't to become my grave.

My gloves filled with water, hindering my grip to the point that it became clear I would stand a better chance without them. With my bare hands, I gripped the ice in a desperate attempt to raise myself up onto the ice again. As I frantically struggled to grasp the jagged ice, my fingers and hands quickly became sliced and bloody, adding a stinging sensation even through the numbness from the incredible cold. As I pulled myself upward, the ice began to submerge an inch or two. Carefully, I lifted one leg up onto the ice, then the other. Slowly, I slid the remaining portion of my weight up onto the ice. For a brief moment, I lay suspended on my new, icy platform, liberated from my watery grave. Then with a loud crash, another giant piece of ice broke off, returning me to the dark waters below.

I could now see the ice was concaved on the underside around the perimeter of the hole due to one of the warm springs in our shallow lake. I knew at this point that any attempt to save myself would prove to be an exercise in futility. With my strength exhausted, the inevitable seemed to loom up before me like an undertaker waiting close by to complete his task.

Until now, the thought of dying had never seriously crossed my mind. Now, truly, my life began to race before my consciousness like a video on fast-forward. Details of my happy childhood came vividly to mind in rapid succession.

My parents had consistently portrayed a warm and inviting picture of God to my sister Sherry and me. My father was the first elder in our church, and my mother always provided leadership for one of the children's departments. From my earliest memories, my parents lived their picture of a loving and kind Father in heaven. My mother and father were often found talking to the God they loved. Our morning and evening family worships were warm and enjoyable moments, providing each of us the opportunity to draw close to God.

From my earliest memories, God was the centerpiece of our home.

I Will Save You to Make You a Blessing

I could not help remembering the special friendship I had enjoyed with God throughout my grade school years. One very pivotal moment in my walk with God came racing through my mind. As a fifth or sixth-grader, I had walked forward to accept Jesus as my Savior in response to the call of a visiting evangelist. Balancing on the brink of eternity, the importance of every other area of my life seemed totally inconsequential.

A Christian education was never considered optional for Sherry and me even though it came with a significant sacrifice for my parents. In a spirit of total unselfishness, our parents often denied themselves in order to ensure the payment of our church school tuition. A classic example of this unselfish spirit was exemplified by my mother's clothes closet. For many months her closet rod supported only two dresses, one for church and one for work.

Another example of her dedication to our family and her spirit of unselfish labor was demonstrated when our washing machine malfunctioned. After many years of service, the spin cycle retired. Day after day my mother wrung out each piece of clothing by hand, never considering our tuition money to be on the bargaining table. Many memories of love flooded my mind. I was so thankful to be a part of a home that was always a cheerful place to be, even when life presented challenges, like broken washing machines, that seemed not to have answers.

We lived three miles from town in a country setting with a few acres that afforded us a small orchard, a large garden, a nice pasture for our horse, as well as our own lakefront access. Three other Christian families purchased the land on either side of us, planting beautiful orchards and gardens, creating a wonderful place to grow up. Next door, Gary and Jim Morgan joined me after school as we built forts, explored the countryside, water-skied, and raced and jumped our bicycles on the trails and racetracks we built together. I had a horse, a dog, and a pet magpie that my mother taught to talk; what more could a boy ask for growing up?

All these wonderful memories flooded my mind as the reality of their sudden end loomed ominously before me. As my life-video came to the current years, I knew that my life was not in harmony with heaven. A transition had gradually taken place in my seventh-grade

Thin Ice

year that had quickly taken me from the peace I had known in earlier years. Some new students coming from a non-Christian home began to attend our little Christian school, somewhat tempering the atmosphere of our classroom.

To be considered cool became my aim and focus, leaving my relationship with Jesus somewhere behind. My pastor, teacher, parents and friends could easily see the changes that were taking place in my life and took every opportunity to encourage me in as many ways as they could. But at this moment I knew I had drifted far from my Saviour's arms of love. I knew that if my life ended at this moment, I would be lost from the eternal home that I had always planned to enjoy. I looked up into the sky and cried out to God, "God if you will somehow save me, I will serve You the rest of my life." Just as I felt that the tug from the powerful unseen force beneath the dark, icy hole would swallow me, I experienced a new surge of strength come into my aching muscles.

My father was a building contractor and had been working the past several months in a nearby town building houses. For some unknown reason, he had been impressed to work on our neighbor's roof that day. He just happened to turn toward the lake at the very moment I plunged through the ice. He raced for the phone to call the fire-rescue squad; the voice on the other end indicated it would take ten or fifteen minutes for them to reach our rural location. He ran back to the house he had been working on with the young Spanish man who was helping him. They grabbed two long two-by-fours and ran for the lake.

The young Spanish man was much lighter than my father and quickly volunteered to attempt a rescue. He lay on his stomach with a two-by-four on either side of him, sliding slowly out to the place where I was bobbing in the icy water. He was able to reach me in just a few minutes, but it seemed more like an eternity to me. With the long two-by-fours extended as far as he could in front of him, he continued to inch his way out to the large hole in the ice that held me captive.

At the very moment I knew I could not hold on another second, the ends of the two-by-fours came inching out across the gaping hole. I frantically grabbed hold with a death grip to the lifesaving boards and began to slowly pull myself up and onto the ice with my last ounce of energy as he maneuvered us in reverse. The ice cracked and groaned beneath the weight of yet another body. The surface of the ice began to sink, causing water to come racing across the top of the ice to greet my rescuer. Courageously, he remained at his task even in the face of the ever present reality that we might both drop back into the icy waters beneath the thin shelf of ice that suspended us.

Slowly, we inched backwards, holding our breath and praying that the fragile layer of submerged ice would hold our weight and we would not both be plunged back into the water, creating an even larger hole. Inch by inch we slid across the watery surface until we were on thicker ice and finally back on solid footing.

Hypothermia had made considerable progress while I was bobbing in the icy waters, making the trip to shore somewhat difficult. With water pouring from my clothing, I finally stepped back on solid ground. Later I would learn that the man who had saved my life did not even know how to swim, but risked his life to save mine. I will never forget his selfless spirit. His valiant rescue in every way defined him as a true hero.

Opening the front door, I left my cold, wet clothes in a pile and headed for a tub of warm water my mother was drawing for me. Never before had a warm tub of water felt so wonderful as that day!

You might say I was fortunate or just plain lucky that my father changed his plans that day. You might say that it sure was a good thing that two, long two-by-fours were quickly accessible and a valiant young man with just the right stature was ready to man them. You might say it was fortunate that the stars were properly aligned in order that my father just happened to be up on the roof facing the lake at the moment I plunged into the water. You may attribute all this to chance, but I will always believe that a loving, Heavenly Father, who orders the events of our lives, was directing in every detail of that memorable day, that He might spare my life. A God who hears the cry of His children, sometimes even before they call, had orchestrated a plan that would give a wayward child another opportunity to chart the course of his life. I will be grateful for an eternity for the privilege to live and testify of a Savior such as Him.

2
With Peter in Pilate's Courtyard

I wish my promises to God in those icy waters had been the beginning of a new course decided for my life. How differently the next few pages of my life would read. I am tempted to skip over the period in my life that I spent running from God, but I know that God can use even the dark moments in our lives to encourage someone else if we provide Him the opportunity. For the benefit of a parent or grandparent, for the benefit of those praying for friends and loved ones who, from every appearance, have gone so far that God could never reach them, I must include the evidence that our God is able to save to the uttermost.

My life very quickly resumed a course that left little or no time for God. I became more determined than ever in my search for what appeared to be a life filled with fun and excitement. I gravitated to those that were living life with abandon, throwing all caution to the wind.

Summer came just a few short months after my promise to God from an icy hole in the lake. How quickly I had forgotten my promise to the God who had spared my life. I am lost in amazement as I attempt to understand why a God of love and kindness continues His relentless pursuit of such ungrateful and rebellious children. I am so grateful that He has never treated me with the indifferent attitude that I treated Him.

Living next to a lake defined the summer months as wonderful times of fun in the sun and water. Evenings and weekends were filled with swimming, boating and skiing. Winter was not the only time the lake became a social gathering place; summers also pro-

I Will Save You to Make You a Blessing

vided many opportunities to enjoy activities with friends and neighbors.

One Sunday afternoon a classmate from school pulled up to the shoreline below our house in a boat with an older friend of his, inviting me to come along for a ride with them. These young men were not the influence that my parents were encouraging by any means. Both of them had gone to church when they were younger but had long since abandoned thoughts of God and His plan for their lives. As I walked down the hill to get into the boat, the language and conversation instantly made me aware of the turn that their lives had taken. I had not been confronted at this point in my life with the company of people that seemed to fit lewd and crude words between each of their other words. As we shoved off from shore and started the motor, I felt so out of place with these older friends who were choosing a path for their life that clearly indicated God was not in their thoughts or plans.

The breeze felt good on that hot summer afternoon as the boat started to glide across the water. It was only a moment until one of them reached in a cooler and pulled out a beer.

"Do you want a beer?" he asked, holding up a can in front of me.

Even though I knew I had not been walking closely with God, the idea of drinking or smoking did not seem all that attractive to me at the time.

"No, thanks," I replied, feeling a little embarrassed but trying to appear cool and in control.

He looked me right in the eye and said, "What's the matter? Are you one of those Jesus boys?"

I felt my face become hot and flushed as the pressure to comply and fit in seemed almost overpowering. I emphatically replied, "NO, I AM NOT. I just don't want one."

They turned around, laughing and drinking their beer, leaving me to my misery in the back seat of the boat. I had never been challenged so directly regarding my relationship with God. Even though I was temporarily out of the spotlight, I felt terribly uncomfortable. After a few moments, the cigarettes came out, and the rock music began to play. They laughed and told crude stories and jokes as they appeared to be having the time of their lives. I wasn't sure why I was feeling so uncomfortable; after all, weren't these the very kids that I thought were having all the fun? Now here I was, right where I thought I wanted to be to enjoy life to the fullest, and I was more miserable than ever. After a few minutes that seemed more like hours, they dropped me off in front of my house and sped away.

It wasn't until later that I realized why I felt so incredibly guilty and uncomfortable that day. The place on the lake that I faced the question concerning my relationship with Jesus was the very spot I had fallen through the ice just a few months before. I had denied that I even knew Jesus on the very spot he had saved my life. I had denied Jesus on the very spot I had promised Him I would be faithful to Him for the rest of my life.

I felt like it was me standing in Pilate's courtyard by the fire that night, not Peter. It was me looking into the loving eyes of a Savior waiting to die for me, and yet, I had denied I even knew Him. I knew how Peter felt standing by the fire with all eyes on him when he was faced with almost the identical question. Only an amazing God filled with an indefinable love would send His Son to die for such an ungrateful sinner; only a loving Savior would continue to stand on the balcony waiting to die for my sins when I denied I ever knew Him.

Over and over again I have experienced only loving responses from a God who defines His love in ways that are beyond my understanding. A lesser god would have ended his pursuit for one in rebellion right from the start.

After attempting a year at Upper Columbia Academy, I enrolled at the local public high school, much to the disappointment of my parents. The next few years were the saddest any parent could ever experience. Very quickly I became alcohol and chemical dependent—smoking, drinking, and using numerous drugs on a regular basis. I became a ward of the court at age 15 after being convicted of several crimes. I spent the next 10 years running from God.

I will not detail the depths that sin takes you when once you abandon light and truth, exchanging them for darkness and lies of deception. I do want you to know the power of your prayers on behalf of the one that looks hopeless and beyond the possibility of ever knowing freedom again. If by sharing this portion of my life even one person gains new insight and courage to intercede for someone that either cannot or will not call heavenward for help, I

I Will Save You to Make You a Blessing

will write it just for you.

Let me encourage you by sharing some of the ways God uses your prayers to reach a loved one wherever they may be. My parents knew how to pray earnestly and fervently with a faith that refused to let go in spite of how they felt or how hopeless the situation appeared. I never came home at night without either my mother or father waiting up for me in prayer and Bible study.

Can you imagine how it feels to come home late at night, opening your front door and stepping into the Godly atmosphere of prayer and Bible study? Each and every time I came home, I would find one or both of my parents in prayer for me with a Bible lying open next to their folded hands. I want to assure you that I knew there was not a place I could hide that would escape their powerful prayers.

I want you to try to picture your loved one at a large party: the music is deafening, everyone is heavily intoxicated, high or both. From every outward appearance, the powers of darkness have so surrounded all in this environment that hope of a spiritual rescue would seem impossible. This would seem to be the last place in the entire universe that you would find a pure and holy God. Because you are home praying, the Creator God of the universe elects to go to the party on your behalf. Your son or daughter hears the same voice I have heard so many times say to them, "Your parents are home praying for you at this very moment."

I want to assure you that it matters not the degree of your unconsciousness or intoxication; when God speaks, you are at that moment very sober and attentive. I have experienced God's voice penetrate the influence of various drugs and alcohol. He has never been intimidated or challenged in the least by these strongest weapons of the enemy of souls.

Over and over this scenario has been repeated in my life. My prayer for the one praying today would be that you could somehow hear the softness, the gentleness, and the deep wooing love that filled every personal entreaty. If you could hear the sweetness of His voice even just once, I know you would never falter in faith again as you intercede on behalf of one that the enemy of God is holding fast as a captive.

I would like to share with you one incident in particular that has always been a powerful reminder of the kind of prayer I mentioned above. A large foosball tournament was being held in one of the local taverns in Moses Lake. Several of my close friends were in the final rounds of competition. The tavern was packed with spectators and participants. The whole atmosphere was filled with loud music, laughter and boisterous conversation. I was sitting on a bar stool facing the tournament when God spoke to me in a most startling and unforgettable way. In clear and direct words that I can hear clearly to this day He said, "HOW LONG HALT YE BETWEEN TWO OPINIONS?" (1 Kings 18:21). The voice was so penetrating and personal that my first response was from reflex rather than thoughtfulness.

I instinctively spun around on my stool to face the one speaking to me; no one was there. I felt the presence of God all around me as I realized the One who had spoken to me was the One who had set fire to the sacrifice of Elijah on Mount Carmel so many years ago, when Elijah challenged wayward Israel with these same words. God could see what no other human being could see in my heart. Down deep inside I wanted to be free once again. I became instantly very sober in the power of a Creator God even though I had spent most of the day trying to hide from a very guilty conscience. For me, the party was over, and I left with deep emotions and the echo of God's words stirring my soul.

The ones who were praying for me never knew until years later what their prayers were doing at this pivotal moment in time, but they never stopped, even when all the evidence pointed to hopelessness. The prayers of consecrated family and church members allowed God the freedom to repeat His entreaties over and over again. God's word says that real, availing power is exerted in the supernatural dimension when those that are consecrated to God pray for the merits of Jesus' shed blood on behalf of another. If the family of God understood even a fraction of the power that would enter the supernatural battlefield as the result of their prayers, I am sure we would be more faithful to bring our loved ones before the throne of grace where we can always find help in every emergency and time of need. If our eyes could be opened to the engagement of God's army in response to powerful intercessory prayer, I am sure we would see one hundred in the weekly prayer meeting where now there is one.

Is there someone in your life that could use a visit from God? Why don't you stop what you are doing for a moment and come before the Father in the merits of Jesus' shed blood on Calvary on behalf of your loved one who is being held hostage by the enemy? Someday soon, you will sing praises with them around the throne in glory, and together we will place our crowns before the One that came to set captives free.

3
The Death Angel Passes By

I wish I could say the beautiful pictures of love that God continued to surround me with caused me to see life from an altogether different perspective. I wish this was the part of the story that said the many loving entreaties from the Lord caused me to return to Him.

Over and over, I encountered a Savior who continued to love me in spite of the way I treated Him. Even though God continually allowed me to experience His love in very personal ways, my lifestyle remained unchanged. For some reason, I was determined to explore the path that promises pleasure and excitement for every traveler. By the time I finished high school I had journeyed far from home on this illusive pathway in search of its reward. The further down this path I went the more I discovered that hopelessness and despair were the only real rewards that could be found.

A few months after graduating from high school, I married a young lady I will call Trudy. We continued a lifestyle of pleasure seeking and parties, continuing to search for the happiness that the world so freely offers. We lived for the first year and a half in Moses Lake, Washington, while I worked on a massive expansion project at Grand Coulee Dam.

During this time, our daughter, Heidi, was born, and our family began. I enrolled in a vocational school for welding and discovered that I had a natural talent that enabled me to begin a career as a pipe welder. Numerous electrical generating power stations under construction in the western states were seeking pipe welders. Consequently, we began a life of traveling from construction site to construction site.

I Will Save You to Make You a Blessing

Occasionally, I would return home for a visit with family and friends. It was on one of these visits that I once again was reminded that there was a God in heaven watching over me. As I exited the highway and made my way into Moses Lake, I met some friends who were on their way to a party.

"Hey, why don't you come along?" one of them called from a parked car. "We are going to a party just out of town. Follow us." I looked forward to seeing friends that I hadn't seen for a while, and a party always seemed like a good idea.

The little house was filled to overflowing when we arrived. Everyone was making a valiant attempt to have a good time, and as is often the case at such parties, all semblance of restraint had disappeared and gone by the wayside. Hour after hour the meaningless routine of illusive pleasure seeking continued; that's when Ken pulled up in his new Chevelle SS.

Ken was a drummer in a rock band, and he loved fast cars. He had just taken his engine to a special high performance shop to have it rebuilt with maximum horsepower. With 425 horses under the hood giving it lightning performance, everyone wanted a ride in his car.

After a few trips up and down the country road, Ken threw me the keys to the car and said, "Do you want to take it for a ride?"

What a question. Of course I did! However, Ken's car and my hours of partying were not a good combination. I had been there for several hours by then and had very poor judgment to be the driver of such a powerful car. Several others jumped in for the ride. With the pedal to the floor, we took off down the road. In seconds we were traveling at speeds of well over a hundred miles an hour. A few miles down the road we stopped and turned around to return to the party. For some reason, when we came to the driveway where Ken was standing, I flew on by; why go back now when we are having so much fun?

About a quarter mile or so past the driveway, the road made a sharp curve to the right. Traveling at incredible speeds, we were in the curve before I knew it. It was too late to slow down or possibly make the turn. The inertia pulled us from the road with the force of a giant magnet. A large telephone pole stood just off the shoulder of the road in the center of the curve. The center of the hood was directly in line with the pole as the tires left the pavement, skidding through the gravel

The Death Angel Passes By

on the edge of the road. Every person in the car froze and held their breath as it appeared it would be their last. Just a split second before impact, something totally miraculous took place.

One moment we were just about to impact the pole, and the next, the car made a right angle turn. We were traveling down the road in the right lane going the right direction and at the correct speed. In an eerie silence, we slowly made our way back to the party.

No one knew what had happened just a moment ago, except me—I knew many caring people were praying. It seemed the harder and faster I ran from God, the more His amazing love surrounded me. The death angel had come again, but the prayers of a loving family and friends availed God yet another opportunity to rebuke the devourer's call.

Another amazing demonstration of love came knocking at my door one day not long after the miracle in Ken's car. I was back in Moses Lake for a brief interim between construction projects. With the smell of marijuana smoke still lingering in the air, the unexpected knock at the door caused my heart to race. With blurry red eyes, I opened the door to find Pastor Johnson standing on the other side.

"I need to talk to you for a moment if I could," he said. I will never forget the power of his brief visit. There was something about the kindness in his eyes and the love in his voice that captivated my attention immediately.

"Greg," he said, "we have waited and waited for you to come back to join our church family. We care about you, and we miss you." For the next moment or two he painted pictures of God's love with words as vivid as any skilled artist might paint with brush and oils on canvas. He reminded me of a God who loved me personally and was longing to restore my lost friendship with Him. The look of genuine love that was written all across his face and the deep compassion in his eyes powerfully moved upon my heart as I listened on in silence.

All at once, tears began to form in his eyes as he stood appealing for my salvation. He said, "Your lifestyle choices indicate your desire to not be included as a church member any longer. We will honor your choice, but we are praying you change your mind soon." He finished by saying, "We want you to know you are welcome back in our church any time you are ready to come back. Please, don't wait too long."

I Will Save You to Make You a Blessing

With tears in his eyes he turned and walked back to his car.

I felt like Jesus had stopped by in person to invite me to spend eternity with Him. My Father in heaven continued to use many of His thousand ways that we know not of to pursue me with one kind and loving invitation after another. Oh, how I pray that every person who receives a visit of this nature might know the genuineness of a family of God, who loves so deeply they weep at the thought that someone's special place in heaven might be vacant.

Friend, are there tears in your eyes for one who no longer worships with you? Perhaps at this very moment God is placing a picture of someone that needs a visit from you as an ambassador for Christ. Perhaps it would make an eternal difference for this special person to see a tear in your eye at the thought that they would not enjoy the special place prepared for them. May God restore in you and me the kind of love and compassion that He has for the lost.

Dustin, our second addition to the family, joined us just before our next move. I learned of a power plant in eastern Montana needing pipe welders, and I needed a job, so the 40-foot trailer was loaded and readied to go. It was all our four-wheel drive pickup could do to pull a trailer equivalent to a semi trailer down the highway.

All went well until we began the steep climb in Idaho, winding slowly up the mountain pass. Nearing the summit of the pass, the road suddenly became glazed with a coat of ice. I could feel the truck beginning to lose traction. As we came around a sharp curve in the road, we peered far down the mountainside to the rocky canyon floor two or three thousand feet below us. The only separation between us and the sheer cliff right beside us was a guardrail that looked very small just then. Our park model trailer sat very high in the air, making it doubtful that such a railing would even slow us down.

Looking at our two young children resting in the seat beside me, I knew our little family was in real trouble. We were losing momentum rapidly, and it was clear that at any moment our forward progress would halt, and a tragic slide in reverse would follow. It seemed that we were all but stopped, holding our breath for the downward plunge that was sure to begin at any moment.

Out of nowhere, a dump truck pulled directly in front of us and began spreading sand onto the highway. Just enough sand came sliding

The Death Angel Passes By

back to our tires to cause us to regain traction without a moment to spare. I do believe we were nearing a velocity of 0 mph when our truck tires encountered the sand and made a new grip with the highway, enabling us to inch our way up to the top of the pass and then down the other side. The timing of this miracle dump truck was too incredible to miss. There is not a doubt in my mind that the death angel came calling again but was turned back because loving family members were praying for one who was running from God.

Friend, do you know someone who needs your prayers? I believe God is waiting for you and me to cooperate in the advancing of His position during these final moments of the raging battle between good and evil on planet Earth. Your prayers might mean life for someone hanging in the balances today!

After a few short months in eastern Montana, an issue with the local labor union arose. My general foreman was one of the union organizers, and I was not a member. He made no pretense about his feelings concerning those that weren't union members. Consequently, he arranged for me to be transferred to a very undesirable position. He was quite sure I would quit; he was right, I did, even though I had not saved any money for such an emergency.

We loaded our things, and with trailer in tow, we began our return journey west to Washington. As I began to calculate our moving expenses, I wished I had been more careful with my money. I had just enough for food and gas to make it back to Moses Lake. It was quite clear there would be no motel stops on this trip.

After just a few hours of driving, a strong wind began to blow from the west. The further we went the stronger the wind blew. By 9:00 p.m. winds with 70 mph gusts had us crawling at a snail's pace. The winds continued to increase by the minute. By 9:30 p.m. we came to a barricade stating that the highway was closed due to extremely high winds ahead. We exited with the other weary westbound travelers. The high winds had cut our gas mileage in half, totally frustrating our already challenged financial status. With a barricade across the highway it looked like continuing would be impossible; there would be no other choice but to find a place to sleep for the night and hope the wind would be gone by morning.

There were few lodging choices in this little town that had all of

I Will Save You to Make You a Blessing

Interstate 90 coming to an unexpected halt at its doorstep. We found a cheap room and collapsed from the stress of the last few hours of travel. We awoke from sleep to the shriek of hurricane-force winds violently blowing all around us. We turned to the weather channel on TV for an update on the conditions and a forecast for the day. The winds were blowing with gusts up to 100 mph without any indication that a change in this ferocious storm might be coming anytime soon. From our window we could see a small café against the backdrop of trees bending over at a right angle just across the parking lot from our motel. As we opened the door to make the short walk to the café, the wind nearly swept us off our feet. It was all we could do to fight our way across the parking lot.

The little café was packed with stranded travelers who literally had nowhere else to go. The highway department had a large barricade all the way across Business 90 stating in bold letters, "Road Closed, extremely high winds ahead." The conversations were all the same: "When are these winds going to quit?" The local people informed us that the wind had been blowing like this for four days. The winds were originating from the mouth of the Yellowstone River Canyon just 50 miles to our west. We were told that once you made it past the huge canyon the winds began to subside almost immediately.

I was more than a little concerned as I kept mentally reviewing the balance sheet of our meager finances. What were we going to do? Back in our room, we sat staring at the wind gauge on TV, watching the needle occasionally hit the 100 mph mark.

A knock at the door interrupted our thoughts and our fixed stare at the wind gauge. It was the owner of the hotel. With a contented smirk on her face she said, "You folks will be with us for another night then, I suppose?" Almost without hesitation I said, "No, we are leaving!"

Her mouth dropped as she turned and faced the tempest behind her. I hadn't even considered driving in this ferocious storm. The words just came out in response to a gleeful hotel owner with all the odds in her favor. I supposed after making a statement like that the only thing to do was leave. If we could just make it those 50 miles, we would be past this terrible storm. I'm not sure what the people in that little café thought as they watched a pickup truck and a 40-foot trailer with a family of four drive around the "Road Closed" barricade and head west down

The Death Angel Passes By

the highway.

The wind violently smashed small stones and sticks against the windshield with such fury we were only able to reach a top speed of 25-30 mph with the accelerator to the floor. A large hill on our left side provided a partial barrier against the hurricane force winds for the first 25 or 30 miles. All at once the road took a little bend to the right and we were out in the middle of the wide open prairie with winds that seemed to blow us around on the highway at will. The winds were mostly side winds now, causing us to be swept violently across all lanes of the highway and down onto the right shoulder. Just as soon as a powerful gust would partially abate, I would steer back over onto the shoulder of the inside lane. Almost immediately, another blast would sweep us to the opposite ditch again. The maximum speed I could obtain was between 15-25 mph, depending on the wind gusts.

It was at this point we came up behind a semi truck and trailer. We had not encountered another vehicle of any kind until now, let alone a semi truck and trailer.

His truck was an even larger kite in the wind. After following him for only a few minutes, we watched in horror as a giant blast of wind twisted the metal of his trailer right before our eyes, bending the box over to one side and then sending him up on one set of tires, bouncing down the road like a small toy on a string. It was not reassuring in the least to be staring at metal bending and twisting directly in front of us. After a moment of balancing and bouncing, the wind took a moment's pause, causing the trailer to come slamming back down to the pavement on all wheels once again.

A feeling of total helplessness completely pervaded the atmosphere. My mind raced over my reckless life which seemed about to come to an end once again. Was this to be the way it would end? Each second seemed like an eternity. Finally, we came to a sign that said "Livingston 7 miles." It felt like we were driving right into the open mouth of this wind dragon. After what seemed to be an eternity, we came to the road sign we had been waiting for: "Livingston next two exits."

Trudy asked, "Which exit are you going to take, the first or the second?" We always tried to avoid going through towns due to the obvious navigational challenges that result from needing sixty feet of traffic space for our truck and trailer. That seemed reason enough to

I Will Save You to Make You a Blessing

skirt cities and towns.

"It's only a couple more miles," I said. "I am going on to the second exit." I moved to the far left side preparing for the next blast of wind. As I approached the first exit, the steering wheel I was gripping with white knuckles and tight muscles turned abruptly to the right as if I weren't even holding the wheel at all, causing us to veer suddenly and unexpectedly to the right.

As we cut abruptly across all lanes of the highway and onto the off ramp, Trudy exclaimed, "I thought you said you were taking the second exit? What was that all about?"

I just drove on in silence realizing that something supernatural had just taken place. We were emotionally exhausted and in a daze as we pulled into the truck stop at the west end of town. This truck stop was just as packed as the one at the other end of the storm, only these weary travelers were waiting on this side of the storm instead of the other.

"Where are you headed?" the man behind the counter asked.

"West," I replied.

"I saw you pull in," he said. "You must know this part of Interstate 90 pretty well."

"Why do you say that?" I asked.

"Because you came through town rather than coming around town; nobody has made it around town in the last four days."

From the window he pointed to a deep canyon carved by the Yellowstone River winding far below. "That canyon with the high mountains on either side of it is the tunnel creating all this wind. The winds coming out of that canyon are reaching gusts up to 140 mph," he said. "You see that bridge over the Yellowstone River? Nobody has been able to make it across that with a trailer in four days now. Good thing you didn't try going around town; you would be at the bottom of that canyon right now."

I walked slowly away in silence as I realized the death angel had come once again, but God turned him away because of the powerful prayers of a loving family. What an incredible picture of a God who never gives up on black sheep who are lost and alone on the mountainside.

The rest of that journey was a quiet and thoughtful ride as I felt the presence of God quietly inviting me back to Him. How anyone could resist such a God as this I really can't imagine, but I did.

I wonder if there is someone you know who is in need of a special invitation from our kind and loving Heavenly Father? Your prayers provide Him with just such an opportunity!

4
Returning to My Father's House

For most of us the parable recorded in Luke 15: 11-32 of a prodigal son is a familiar passage of scripture. If you have not recently read the account of a son that spurned his father's love, demanding his inheritance well in advance of his father's death for the purpose of riotous living, you may want to review it. It is one thing to read this story and another to live it.

Deep in my heart I knew I was the son who had gone to a far country in search of a life of pleasure and excitement. I had squandered many years searching for the illusive mystique that I thought danced behind neon lights. The laughter that at one time sounded like someone having the time of his life, now sounded very empty and hollow. I realized I could no longer ignore the haunting loneliness of a heart that had tried so desperately to find meaning and happiness without God. The music that so powerfully drew me at first, now sounded artificial and meaningless. The substances that I at first thought would take me to some wonderful high, left me struggling to even feel normal, whatever normal was; I just wasn't sure any more. The road to a far country that I thought would lead to freedom, pleasure, and happiness had instead led me to an existence that could easily be likened to the pig pen of the prodigal son.

Financial destitution is only one resource that a kind and loving Father has at His disposal. When God opens your eyes to the stark reality of a life intent on pleasure-seeking, it is like someone lifting a large curtain that has hidden all the degradation, woe, and sorrow from sight. Truly, when sin is unmasked it looks, tastes, and smells

Returning to My Father's House

like a pen filled with swine and its subsequent residue.

The reality of my condition and the constant barrage of guilt provided a very miserable state of existence. My mind began to feel so taxed and overloaded with the weight of sin that it started sending messages of warning to my body. It was impossible for me to relax. Restful sleep became less and less frequent. I could relate so well with the scripture that says, "In the morning thou shalt say, Would God it were even! and at even thou shalt say, Would God it were morning! For the fear of thine heart wherewith thou shalt fear" (Deuteronomy 28:67).

This very appropriate description of my days and nights left me in an increasingly exhausted state of mind. The struggle became so intense that my whole body began to tingle and itch. I concluded that something had drastically gone wrong with some internal organ, and it was time to seek the help of a medical professional. I randomly selected a clinic that would accept a new patient and made an appointment.

After giving me a complete physical, the doctor looked me straight in the eyes and said, "There is not a thing wrong with your health. I believe your problem is of a completely different nature." He said, "Tell me, were you raised in a Christian home?"

I quietly replied, "Yes."

He then asked me a very pointed question. "Is your life surrendered to Jesus as your Lord and Savior today?"

I looked at the floor as I said, "No."

He said, "Do you want me to tell you what I believe your problem is?"

"Yes, I need to know," I replied. I will never forget the kindness that shone through the eyes of a physician I had never seen before as he spoke on behalf of his Savior.

He said, "Jesus is coming back very soon to take all of His children home, and you are not ready for Him to come. Your conscience is so full of guilt that your whole nervous system is literally on edge, giving you this pins and needles sensation."

I left the visit to a random medical clinic realizing once again that a loving Father was not willing to spend eternity without me. He had spoken another loving entreaty through a kind physician who had com-

I Will Save You to Make You a Blessing

mitted his life to healing, both physically and spiritually.

I knew the choices I thought would lead to a life of fun and excitement had in reality made me a prisoner. I was addicted and held fast by chains that would not let me go. When you begin to come to your senses, the pig pen loses its appeal in a hurry. It takes very little thought to conclude that you would like to leave as soon as possible. When you look around for a way out you find you are mired too deeply in the muck, and the pen has no gate to allow an exit. This reality became a haunting reminder that life in my Father's house was a life filled with real meaning and joy, but I didn't know how to find my way back home. I'm so thankful for the kind and patient Father who has a thousand ways that we are never aware of, all of which lead us back to His house. He had just such a plan already in place for my life.

I learned of a fabricating shop in Portland, Oregon, that was hiring pipe welders for the Alaskan pipeline. They had a large contract to fabricate the piping systems for the pumping stations that were located all along the Alaskan pipeline. With trailer and family I was off to Portland.

As I began this job, I was glad to learn that it would be a lengthy project creating some much-needed stability. The climate in Portland was a refreshing change, and the landscape was beautiful. Just when it seemed like this would be our home for an extended period of time, the supply of pipe and materials became unavailable literally overnight causing the fabricating shop to close its doors until the materials were available once again. Now what would we do? Everything was going wrong all at once, it seemed. I called all over the western United States looking for a job. It became painfully clear that at that moment there were none.

As I felt the mounting pressures of growing financial responsibilities, I heard a still, small voice suggest calling my father in Wisconsin. My father and mother had moved to Wisconsin to build some much-needed churches and schools the year I graduated from high school. I knew I had to do something soon, so I called to see if my father could use my help. He assured me that he had plenty of work, and I could begin immediately if I wanted to come.

I didn't know it right then, but my Father in a far country was arranging a way for me to escape the pig pen, and He had chosen to

Returning to My Father's House

use my earthly father to carry out His plan. Both of my fathers had spent the last several years together patiently watching the horizon day and night for the lonely figure of a lost son making his way back home. It is important for me to add that my father never stood alone at the side of the road. My mother never left that lonely roadside for even a moment for many long years as well. My sister joined the Father and other horizon watchers. I am told my grandmother sometimes waited all night watching in the darkness with the Father. Joining the watchers from time to time were aunts, uncles, cousins, and a host of church family members.

It was a long drive from Portland, Oregon, to Madison, Wisconsin. I had plenty of time to think and evaluate my life thus far as I drove hour after hour across Interstate 90. I knew working with my father in Wisconsin and living in my parents' Christian home would be a drastic change from the lifestyle I had been living, but I also knew I was ready for a change. I did not have to wait long before discovering that the one that had been so ruthlessly holding me captive was not about to let me go without a fight.

I had not gone far when an amazing struggle for my soul began to take place. A distinct voice began commanding me to turn around and go back. "You will hate it there. You know you won't be free to do all the things you love to do once you get there." In response another voice full of kindness reminded me of the longing in my heart to be set free and promised, "Your parents will help you find your way back to Me." This argument went on and on hour after hour, mile after mile, but could not be heard by anyone but me. It was so distinct to me, however, that as time went on I could even begin to recognize the difference in the personalities of the beings that were arguing for my soul. The desire for a life of real freedom, combined with such amazing, loving entreaties, caused me to press on, even against the onslaught of spiritual attacks.

An ice storm, beginning in Minnesota and continuing into Wisconsin, glazed the highways with about a half an inch of ice, creating a perfect climax for one long journey that had turned out to be an incredible battle. Climbing out of our truck and walking through the door to my parents' home felt like one big sigh of relief.

My mother immediately began using her evangelistic skills in the

I Will Save You to Make You a Blessing

kitchen. A delicious home-cooked meal can preach a wonderful sermon! If God has blessed you with this special gift, use it as an evangelistic tool at every possible opportunity to further advance the gospel and hasten the soon return of our Savior.

Returning to a home filled with the atmosphere of Jesus flooded my mind with memories of the life I left so long ago. I knew instantly that my Heavenly Father had rescued me from a pig pen existence and was bringing me home.

Evangelistic meetings soon began in the church my parents were attending, and Trudy and I were invited to attend with them if we should choose to. As soon as I stepped into the house of God, the warmth of His presence spoke to the loneliness of my heart. I knew He had heard and understood my unspoken cries for help from a "far country." At the close of the meetings, Trudy and I answered a call for those desiring to surrender their lives to Jesus as Lord and Savior. We joined others as they came forward in response to a call for baptism.

As I walked down that aisle I knew I was the prodigal coming home with nothing but wretched, filthy rags for a covering. As the prayer of dedication was offered for each of us in the front, I felt the Father wrap His clean robe of righteousness around me, covering a lifetime of sinful rags. Only one that has been dressed in rags can know the joy of such a covering. I could almost hear my Heavenly Father calling his servants, the angels, to bring me some clean sandals and a royal signet ring for my finger. I didn't even deserve the status of servant, but the King of the universe had just declared me royalty. Who could resist such a loving God?

My father had just completed the church that the meetings were being held in a few months before our arrival. Little did he know as he built the baptistery that the ones he had prayed so long and earnestly for would be some of the first to step into its waters. It was truly a fatted calf celebration; the son from a far country had come home at last. We all knew this celebration was not just being celebrated in Wisconsin; the scriptures promised that a celebration in heaven was taking place as well.

I felt free at last. Sinners carry such an amazingly heavy burden that they don't even realize how heavy it really is until they come to the One who says, "Why don't you let Me carry your heavy load from now

Returning to My Father's House

on. You don't ever need to carry it again." I felt like I left an amazing load of guilt and sin in the waters that day, but the struggle was not over. The addictions I had spent years developing did not disappear over night. Every time I would pass by a billboard advertising some form of liquor my mouth would fill with saliva, and I would have to pray for strength from above to come and fight a battle that I was incapable of winning on my own.

I am so thankful for a Savior who left heaven with a very specific task in mind; "to loose the bands of wickedness, to undo the heavy burdens, and to let the oppressed go free, and that He would break every yoke" (Isaiah 58:6). I had to learn to let the One who knew no defeat in the battle with sin and the devil come and do the fighting for me. My Father promised me if I would follow Him, I would never need to feed on the pods in the pig pen again. Oh, how good it felt to be home.

Is there someone you love and care about that has gone to a far country in search of pleasure and excitement? Have they been gone for some time now and you aren't really sure if the Father even remembers they're missing? I want to assure you, the one you care about has never escaped the watchful eye of the One who gave His life for him on Calvary. He stands faithfully watching the horizon waiting for the first glimpse of the tattered and worn figure of your lost and lonely loved one. The one that, from all outward appearances, seems to be gone from home forever, never to return, might be coming to his senses at this very moment. As we pray for God to send heavenly light to illuminate the darkened minds of our loved ones, He is well able to open their eyes to the reality of the pig pen as well. Let's not ever forget that our God knows how to save to the uttermost! Continue to faithfully send your prayers heavenward. Someday you will actually see how much availing took place as the result of those prayers.

5
Weeping May Tarry for a Night, but Joy Cometh in the Morning

A very caring church family in Madison, Wisconsin, included our little family right away, making us feel loved and appreciated. We began helping with youth ministries and activities that enabled us to make the necessary social transition, replacing our past activities with wholesome and innocent fun. God began to rapidly recreate and restore areas in our lives that needed the healing touch of a Creator God. Another baby boy, Seth, joined our family. This new gift of life, together with our new life in Christ, provided many happy moments as our family grew both physically and spiritually. My parents were happy for the time to be with their grandchildren, and all seemed to go well for a while.

Almost without warning, our happy, peaceful world came caving in. Trudy had grown up in a very dysfunctional home with two alcoholic parents. One of the big reasons she chose to get married so young was to escape from a home that had so many sad memories. This new lifestyle appealed to her in many ways at first, but more and more frequently she began to experience mixed emotions concerning the Christian lifestyle. She would sometimes get a faraway look in her eyes and say, "I don't know if I want to live like this for the rest of my life." She struggled with these thoughts off and on for a couple of years until she received an invitation in the mail for a family wedding back in Moses Lake. After a couple of days with old friends and the old lifestyle, she decided she would move back and resume her previous way of life.

I was totally unprepared for the emotional trauma that always comes as a result of a separation and divorce. God says in Malachi

Weeping May Tarry, but Joy Cometh

2:16, "I hate divorce" and I agreed wholeheartedly. I had only one direction to look, up to the One who had so faithfully directed me this far.

"Now what am I supposed to do, Lord?" I asked. "All of a sudden I am a single dad with three children to care for. Lord, I know You have been with me until now; please help me make it through this experience that feels so dark and lonely," I cried. Many a night my pillow became moistened with tears as loneliness and rejection flooded my mind. In my despair I was so thankful for such a loving and supportive family.

My sister, Sherry, had preceded us in migrating to Wisconsin from the state of Washington. Sherry always tried to find creative ways to make the void of a missing mother less painful to her little niece and nephews. A better tea party or picnic designer could not be found anywhere. God truly blessed the little broken hearts of Heidi, Dustin and Seth with her many gifts of love. From the first, our children knew they had a loving Aunt Sherry. In spite of my feelings of loss and pain, I was so thankful God provided such an atmosphere of love and kindness for my children.

Just after we moved to Madison, Lesa, a young lady with two small children, began attending the church that had so graciously adopted our family. As she studied the Bible, she was convicted that she wanted to surrender her life completely to Jesus and was soon baptized. Her husband did not share her enthusiasm for God. He continued to party without her. When he discovered a third baby would soon be joining their family, he started making other plans for his life.

A couple of months after Trudy moved back to Washington, Lesa's husband made his final decision to end his marriage and move to Florida. It was a long and challenging year for both of us. Our new church family did everything they could to let us know they would help in any way they could.

When it became apparent that neither of our spouses would be returning due to other relationships, we began considering a closer friendship. However, when thoughts of developing a closer relationship would pass through our minds, they were usually put in check rather quickly as the implications of such a large family loomed up before us. The thought of six children all under seven years of age seemed to us a rather impossible obstacle that would be nearly insurmountable! Both

I Will Save You to Make You a Blessing

of us began to pray, "Lord, our families have been through so much pain and heartache. Please don't allow our feelings to lead us into a relationship that would only complicate our lives and add even more pain and heartache for the lives of our children." As we prayed for wisdom, the Lord continued to blend our hearts with a very special love. More than once, we said, "Lord, are You sure You are telling us to keep moving forward in this relationship?"

As we considered blending our families, my parents received a call to go to Africa as missionaries. We both could sense that God was leading us to join our two families into one. His peace promised that He would help us through every challenge that would come our way. We could feel a wonderful love growing in our hearts. The Creator was recreating love in two hearts which had thought pain might be the only reality they would know for the rest of their lives.

Our wedding was one for the record books. It was quite a sight for eight people to be joining their lives in one marriage ceremony. Standing next to Lesa was Jacqlyn (in her grandma's arms) age 9 months; Rachel, age two and a half; and Sasha, age five. Standing next to me was Seth, almost three; Dustin, almost five; and Heidi, age seven. Friends from church made comments like, "I can't wait to see how you guys are going to do this?" It was so reassuring to sense God's presence and realize He was creating a union that would honor Him, and we knew He would create a way where it seemed there could be no way.

We moved just south of Rockford, Illinois, to the little town of Rochelle just one month after our wedding. We found a house with just enough bedrooms for two occupants per room, and the fun began. We prayed as we came to the door of this new home, "Lord, please come and fill this house with Your presence and give us wisdom to join all these little lives into one family."

Every morning and each evening we would join for songs of praise and stories from the Bible. The worship hour became a favorite time as each one was encouraged to be part of the evening worship-drama hour acting out stories, imitating animals, singing songs, and many other activities that made discovering God an adventure. We planned as many fun activities for the family as possible. We spent lots of time hiking, canoeing, swimming at the pool, camping, picking berries in the summer, and playing in the snow in the winter.

Weeping May Tarry, but Joy Cometh

For five years we lived in Rochelle, Illinois, learning to make a game of the challenges and looking for the fun that comes from joining so many lives together. Our children were all able to attend a church school in Rockford that further encouraged their understanding of God. We looked forward to school programs and plays that allowed us to see our little stage stars in so many humorous roles. Truly, God was leading and blessing. As time went on, I developed some very serious doubts concerning the philosophy implied in the play "Cheaper by the Dozen." One of the men at work was teasing me just before Lesa and I were married saying, "Does Lesa own a shoe factory?" Soon after we were married, I wished that it hadn't been a joke. Our friends told us of a TV series that was airing at that time called "Eight Is Enough." I am not sure what they could have been talking about, but this much I was sure of; nine would be too many!

Truly, God had wiped away our tears and given us new reasons to sing. Weeping did tarry through a period of darkness in our lives, but most certainly God had given us a joyful morning experience and a new song to sing as He opened the door to a new life of service and happiness.

6
Troubled By Spirits of Darkness

It seems important for those living in a world that has been bombarded with spiritualism to include this part of our story as a means of encouragement to those who are dealing with supernatural powers of darkness. Spiritualism seems to be manifesting itself in epidemic proportions as our world rushes to the climax of a war that started so many years ago in heaven. Many reading this story will most certainly face such powers before the conflict reaches its conclusion on planet Earth. As I write this portion of our story, I am praying that you will find new courage as a Christian caught in a very real battle that is usually fought in a dimension we cannot see or hear. More and more frequently, portions of this battle are crossing over from the invisible to our sphere. The devil would have Christians fearful of his power, not fully realizing the power of the mighty conqueror they have chosen as their leader.

We knew from almost the first night in our new home that we had visitors from the supernatural world that would have loved to destroy us. I am thankful that just as God drew the boundary lines in the battle for Job, He never allowed the spirits of darkness to harass our children. The enemy did not want this family to be happily growing in their walk with God. One night soon after we were married and each of the children had fallen asleep, a fierce lightning and thunderstorm began to crash and boom all around us. We were tired and decided to get some much-needed rest as well. We knelt by our bed and prayed once again for the blessing of God on our new home. We praised Him for both the new reasons to smile and the help He had promised for the challenges that were sure to come in the days and weeks ahead. We prayed one of

Troubled By Spirits of Darkness

those routine prayers for protection from heaven rather than a real earnest and focused petition for safety as we rested for the night. We finished our prayer and climbed into bed, with the commotion of the thunder and a brilliant light show flashing through the window.

Within minutes, another kind of commotion began on the inside of our home as we realized that we were not alone in our room. Spirits of darkness almost always use fear as one of their strongest tactics to try to intimidate humans. Our room seemed to be full of beings surrounding our bed. An almost overwhelming sense of fear swept over both of us. The little hairs on our arms, legs and neck stood on end. Soon, it felt like we could feel breathing on us in the darkness.

This was a totally new experience for both of us. Hour after hour we stared into the darkness expecting at any moment we would see the faces of the beings breathing their hellish breath on us. Morning eventually came, and we began our day with very tired, red eyes.

Some nights we were able to rest throughout the night without any problems, for which we were grateful; other nights the clocks would stop at the hour our visitors arrived, announcing their intent to harass. Sometimes, objects like toys would fall from shelves, crashing to the floor. Sometimes we would feel strong hands push down violently on our bed, causing us to bounce up and down. Sometimes, we would feel strong hands tighten around our necks. Always, we would pray to God for angels of light to come and guard us in our bedroom-turned-battlefield.

We decided if these demons were not going to allow us to sleep, then we would read from the Bible or other inspired writings on the life of Christ. I reached up to the lamp hanging over our bed and turned on the light. We opened *The Desire of Ages*, a wonderful commentary on the life of Christ, and began to read. In only a matter of moments the light bulb slowly began to unscrew in the socket, causing the arcing of electricity, and we were in darkness. The scenario of nightly visits and harassment continued intermittently for several months.

We prayed, asking God to show us if there were any areas in our lives that were creating an open door for these spirits. We had chosen not to have a TV, and we were careful in the music we listened to. Our books, magazines and games were not of a nature that could provide any such opening. We had to just trust God and wait for His deliver-

I Will Save You to Make You a Blessing

ance. We read a few articles from Christian bookstores on the topic, but our situation seemed to get worse rather than anything that might remotely resemble deliverance.

One night we called my aunt, Hazel Burns, in Ohio for some much-needed advice. She listened carefully to the activities that were disrupting our lives. She said, "Let me share some insights with you that I have just discovered myself. I have been studying with a family that has been actively involved in the occult for several years and now are trying to break free.

"We discovered that the more materials we read from deliverance ministries the worse our situation became. I would advise you to stop reading anything from deliverance ministries. As far as possible, don't even talk about the things going on. The devil loves to be center stage, and he will take attention in any form he can get it. He also knows that if he can keep your attention on him, he has taken your eyes from the Savior." She said, "Fill your home with the music of powerful hymns and praise songs that focus on the blood of Jesus and His victory on Calvary. The devil cannot stand to stay anywhere that the sacrifice that defeated him is constantly being lifted up."

She advised us to carefully and prayerfully reexamine every area of our lives, praying for the Holy Spirit to reveal anything the devil could claim as rightful territory and a reason to be in our home. She reminded us that Satan was a defeated foe, and he had not been actually able to do anything to us except annoy and harass us thus far because God had not allowed him to. She said she would be praying for us. We said goodbye and hung up the phone. We did not have long to wait to try out the new plan of action she had suggested.

One night not long after our phone call, the same spirits came back for their nightly entertainment. We prayed for wisdom and courage to follow the advice God had blessed us with. Our first hymn of praise began rather weakly in the face of our supernatural enemies. It was a wonderful feeling to feel the power of God, and the volume of our song begin to grow. Truly, there is "power in the Blood."

The prayer that the Holy Spirit impressed Lesa to pray next found its way right to the mark. "Lord," she prayed, "we are your children. We know that You are the one in charge of our lives, not these evil spirits. We are exhausted and desperately need to rest. We are going to

Troubled By Spirits of Darkness

lay down and go to sleep. Lord, if You allow these demons to stay here all night that's up to You, but we are going to sleep." We laid our heads on our pillows and a sweet sleep came quickly. The rest of the night we slept in peace. Almost as quickly as these spirits had come they were gone, and we did not have to deal with them in this same way again.

I am praying that our experience will help someone dealing with problems of a similar nature. Someone else may find our experience helpful as they minister to others struggling against supernatural forces of darkness. I have discovered that the simple formula suggested by Hazel gives incredible victory in any area of temptation and sin. Let's align our lives fully with the Captain of the Lord of Hosts, because He has promised that if we do, He will make us more than conquerors. I would also remind you of the victory that Jesus experienced as He used memorized scripture to defeat His enemy in the wilderness. You may want to memorize powerful portions of scripture that will become a ready answer to any and all forms of temptation that will come your way. It worked for Jesus in His battles with the devil, and He has promised that it will avail the same power to His children, even unto the end of the world.

More Spiritual Warfare

As we got better acquainted in the little church we were attending I came to know a young man I will call Terry. It was evident that he was really struggling. He invited me to come over to his house one evening to study and pray with him. After a few moments, the real burden weighing him down began to flow out of his heavy heart. He proceeded to share an abbreviated version of his life with me. He married soon after high school to a friend he dated and partied with in school. They felt empty and alone in a meaningless cycle of parties.

One day they received an invitation to attend some evangelistic meetings in their home town. Night after night they learned of a Savior who came on a very costly journey to invite whosoever will to accept an invitation to spend eternity with Him. Jesus filled their lives with many new reasons to smile. At the conclusion of the meetings they were baptized.

He said, "I know Christianity is the right way to go, but it doesn't seem to work for me. I feel like such a hypocrite at church because of my constant failures. I have been through the cycle of failure and defeat so many times I don't want to count them. I am addicted to smoking pot, and I know it." With a sigh he said, "I have promised myself over and over that this will be my last joint, but there is always one more. I am an artist and I love to paint. Come down into my basement and look at my studio."

We walked down the stairs and into a large room with numerous paintings in various stages of completion. He said, "Whenever I have any free time, I come down here and work on one of these paintings. I have always listened to music while I paint as a means of artistic inspiration, so the first thing I do is turn on the 'tunes.' I know rock music isn't good to listen to, but it puts me in the mood to paint. I'm sure there must be some sort of power in the music because after a few minutes, I get this irresistible urge to get high. I go to my stash, roll a joint, and the rest is history. I spend the rest of the night smoking and painting. My wife has had about all she can take of this and is threatening to leave me if I don't make some changes in my life soon."

We looked at the repeating sequence and the individual steps of this cycle of defeat. Looking back at the first steps of a spiral that always led to defeat, it seemed that rock music played a key role in undermining any resolve he tried to maintain.

He said, "I know music is more than entertainment. A friend of mine that I sometimes get high with told me, 'When I listen to one of the local hard rock stations, I hear voices telling me to kill myself. When I'm driving my car, sometimes I hear voices scream at me to drive into the water or into a concrete column along the highway. When I turn on the radio I can actually feel a force taking away my mind.'" Terry concluded, "He doesn't know what is going on and is planning to go for some counseling. I know that this power that he described is the same one that comes to me with the irresistible desire to get high."

We spent a few evenings talking about the power of the gospel, allowing Jesus to come and do the fighting for us, the power of the Word of God, the importance of prayer, and the way to enjoy a life of victory. Terry seemed to understand the principles well enough but just could not bring himself to the place of making a full surrender. God used a very dramatic wake up call for Terry not long after.

Troubled By Spirits of Darkness

As Terry and his partner (linemen for the telephone company) drove along the countryside in their service truck, they received a call from their dispatcher: "The sheriff's department has requested some assistance responding to a suspicious car parked along the road. There is a deputy en route who will meet you at the location designated." They recognized the county road to be one nearby and quickly drove to the location they were given. They easily spotted the sheriff's patrol car parked several car lengths behind a car that appeared to be abandoned alongside the road. They pulled up behind the patrol car and walked up to meet the waiting officer. Together the three of them walked up to the car that had been reported as suspicious.

Terry later told us, "As we approached this abandoned looking car, we felt an amazing, evil presence surrounding us. It was so overpowering it was impossible to miss." He said, "Every hair on my body was standing on end. We carefully approached the car from either side. We were not prepared for the sight that met our eyes. A small boy about four years old lay motionless in the back seat with multiple stab wounds to his little body. A young lady lay slumped and motionless in the front seat. Apparently she had turned the large knife—lying on the seat beside her—on herself, attempting to cut her wrists and then her neck."

Terry said, "We were gagging and on the verge of throwing up from the horrific scene and the overpowering influence that seemed to be everywhere. A feeling of total helplessness swept over us as we waited for the ambulance to arrive. It was all we could do to check for vital signs of the victims because of the overpowering sensation of evil beings all around us. The little boy had no pulse and was not breathing. The young lady had a faint pulse and some rapid, shallow respirations. We stayed until the ambulance arrived, but as soon as we were relieved, we headed for home with very sick stomachs."

Terry came over to our house that evening a shaken, pale-faced young man. He recounted the gory details as they replayed in his mind (most of which I have chosen not to include). God had been speaking to him about the events of the afternoon, giving him a whole new perspective of the war he was fighting inside and the ruthless master that wanted his soul. As he finished relating his horrific experience, he turned and walked out to his car in a daze. We prayed that God would be able to

I Will Save You to Make You a Blessing

use this terrible tragedy to reach Terry before he became a helpless prisoner in his lifestyle of defeat.

As I knelt to pray that night, I heard the Lord tell me He wanted me to go visit the lady that Terry had helped earlier in the day. I said, "Lord, is this really You telling me to go and visit this lady in the hospital?" I went to sleep thinking about the strange instructions I had just received from the Lord. As I studied and prayed early the next morning, the impression to visit this lady continued to grow. Throughout the day I thought of all the reasons why visiting this lady would be impossible.

Because of the nature of the crime and the resulting publicity, I knew it would be impossible to gain access to her room. I wondered, if I did go, what I would say. That evening, I told Lesa of the growing impression to visit the lady Terry told us about the day before. Lesa joined me in prayer asking for wisdom and guidance from above. On Friday morning in prayer I said, "OK, Lord, if you want me to go I will go, but You will have to tell me what You want me to say, because I don't have any idea what to say."

Friday evening, our little family circle met in prayer, earnestly praying for light from heaven for a lady none of us had ever seen before. I walked out the door to go get in the car; almost immediately I realized I was being surrounded by demonic spirits of darkness. Before I could even get to the car, their bold commands began. Like a shout in my ear came the command, "Go back in the house! Who do you think you are, going to visit this lady? She belongs to me!" As I shut the car door, it felt like the entire car was full of this presence. The familiar tingling of the spine, and the hair on my neck and arms that had come to full attention, verified the presence of my unwanted companions. I felt like Martin Luther when he was visited by these powers, reminding him of a long list of sins. "Turn around, go home, you are no saint, what do you think you are doing anyway?" commanded the demons. The commands became increasingly urgent the closer I got to the hospital.

I am so thankful the Lord did not ask me to ride alone in the car that night. He let me know He was right there beside me as well. After several minutes of continuous bombardment from fallen angels of darkness God spoke so boldly from His word that a new power came over me. God said, "I have not given you the spirit of timidity but of power

Troubled By Spirits of Darkness

and love and self control" (2 Timothy 1:7). Every time the devils would issue a new command, the Lord would repeat the words from scripture, filling my mind with a new courage to press on.

This conversation, that went from one voice to the other, became so real that I felt like one of those cartoon characters with an angel of darkness speaking into one ear and an angel of light speaking into the other. By the time I reached the parking lot of the hospital, it felt like the forces of darkness were insistent that I would not reach the one they were holding hostage in despair and darkness. I felt weak and faint from the forces that were assailing me, but God continued to remind me that He had not given me a spirit of weakness but of power, love, and self control. I took a deep breath, filling my lungs with the cold night air, very thankful for the little, praying circle at home, and headed for the main entrance to the hospital.

I walked to the information desk to inquire the room number and walked to the elevator across the hall. The room I needed to reach was on the top floor that had a secured ward in one wing. As the door closed and the elevator started upward, the oppression became so strong I began to feel weak and about to faint. I reached for the elevator buttons and aborted the upward direction, then headed quickly out into the parking lot, gasping for some of the cool, night air. I stopped about halfway to the car and cried out to God. I said, "Lord, You have invited me here to speak on Your behalf. I am here, but I am no match for the powers that are warring against me. I know You are stronger than these defeated demons. I am going back into the hospital in obedience to Your command. I am turning this battle over to You. In the powerful name of Jesus, the mighty conqueror, I entrust my life."

I turned and walked decidedly for the door to the hospital. As I passed through the doors, all sensations of oppression remained outside. It felt like I had just walked through some kind of invisible, spiritual barrier created by an all powerful God. I felt a total freedom as I walked toward the elevator. This time, I noticed a small flower shop in the lobby that I had not seen as I entered only a moment earlier. I stopped and purchased a small bouquet of flowers and returned to the elevator.

As the door opened, I earnestly called out to God, "Lord, I am here because You told me to come, but I still don't have any idea what I will say to the one You want me to visit." The elevator reached the top

I Will Save You to Make You a Blessing

floor, the door opened, and I walked to the double doors that divided Sue's wing from the rest. Just in front of the double doors, I could see the nurses' station at the front of two long hallways. I looked at the room numbers above each room trying to locate the number I had been given. I spotted her room number directly across from the nurses' station.

The location of Sue's room would make it almost impossible for anyone to enter unobserved. Being directly across from the nurses' station would definitely create a challenge. I wondered how I would ever be able to gain access to her room. Just at that moment, each nurse turned with a clipboard and began to walk down the long hallways with their backs to me. I quickly and quietly slipped through the doors, across, the hall and into her room.

At that moment God whispered to me, "Tell her that I love her." God brought me on this special tactical mission to tell one of His wounded children that He loved them, not because of who they were, but because of who He was. The lights were all off, and it took me a second or two to readjust to the dim light shining from the hallway.

Sue lay in the darkness, her arms suspended in traction with bandages from her hands to her elbows. Her head and neck were totally bandaged, making her look more like a mummy than a patient. She stared blankly into the darkness in kind of a numb, shock-like trance. It seemed like I was looking at a torn and broken body that had somewhere shed the inner soul and all purpose for living.

"Do you like flowers?" I asked.

Without blinking or any eye movement, she continued to stare into the darkness as she whispered, "I used to."

I walked over and placed the flowers on a little stand in the general direction she was staring. At that moment, I felt a Savior's love for one of His children who was hurting beyond tears. I said, "I am a friend of one of the men who found you in your car. I am here because your Father in heaven told me to come and tell you He loves you." For a moment or two I told her of a Savior's love that knew no bounds and then promised to come back for a visit another day. I went back to visit Sue several times in the next few weeks. I told her more and more about the Savior who loved her and had died for her.

Troubled By Spirits of Darkness

One haunting question came up over and over again in our visits. "I loved little Andy so much. How could I have done this to him?" she asked. Her little boy was the most precious thing in the entire world to her. She had very few memories of the incident that had so violently stolen her little boy from her. At one point, she made a reference to "they" taking the life of her little boy.

As soon as her wounds healed, she was transferred to a psychiatric ward in another hospital. On my first visit to this new hospital for those with mental illnesses, I was reminded of the depravation sin has caused and how wonderful it will be when all is made new again. After clearing security at the front desk, I passed through the prison-like doors and down the hall to Sue's room. As the Holy Spirit impressed, I continued to unfold more and more of the amazing war that began in heaven but now plagued our planet in such drastic ways.

After several visits to the psychiatric ward, she greeted me very sadly one day. She said, "My psychiatrist (of atheistic persuasion), feels that all this talk of God and a devil is causing me to become confused." She said very sadly, "My doctor said you can't come to visit me anymore, but I want you to know how much your visits have meant to me. I will never forget you."

I was forced to comply with the system, but I continued to pray that the love of God would reach Sue's heart in a saving way and that she would someday be reunited with her precious little Andy in a place where there would be nothing that would "hurt or destroy in all My holy mountain" (Isaiah 65:25).

Never again would I read the headlines of some horrific crime and wonder what would cause someone to behave so much like demons. The fact is, demons are more and more frequently taking control of those that have not accepted the sacrifice of Jesus and allowed Him to become their Savior. I am so thankful for the precious blood of Jesus that stands as a barrier of armor between us and the powers of darkness. God is asking all that are enlisted in His army to fight valiantly, and He promises, "For I have not given you a spirit of timidity, but of power and love and self control" (2 Timothy 1:7).

7
Lord, If We Could Choose

We knew a move would be coming soon, as the nuclear plant I was working on in Illinois was nearing completion. "Lord, we have clearly seen that You have brought us this far. Please show us the next step in our journey with You," we prayed as we considered where to go next. Five years seemed to have literally disappeared. We knew that the God who had so faithfully met our every need would not forget us now.

One day, just before lunch, Lesa initiated a little game with the kids entitled "What I would do if I won a million dollars?" Entries of various pets, toys, and other such dream items appropriate for small children came rolling in. They were playing the game with gusto, inspired by a recently received sweepstakes mailing—after all, the form stated that we were finalists and almost sure winners. In the minds of our small children, the picture of a man knocking on our doorstep holding the coveted prize was a reality not to be taken lightly. Financial planning is important, and much consideration is needed when considering the dispersion of one's first million dollars.

After playing along for a while Lesa said, "Now let's choose the perfect place to live." She said, "Let's write down all the things we would like for our new house to have and what the setting would be if we could choose." The entries started to come faster than her pen could write.

"I want to live in the country."
"I would like some woods to play in."
"I want a stream running through the woods."

Lord, If We Could Choose

"I want horses and a barn."

"I want some trails to ride our little motorcycle on."

"I want a long driveway with a big yard; some big trees with a swing."

"I want a place for a garden."

The list became more and more complex as it grew. Lesa said, "I want an old farmhouse with hardwood floors." With the last dream entry recorded, the list was tucked away and lunch began. The little folded piece of paper was long forgotten by the time our move was planned and the boxes were packed and ready to go.

I decided to open a small welding business in Wisconsin to avoid the constant moves that construction projects required. We shared our plan with Lesa's parents while visiting them one weekend on their farm near Stoughton, Wisconsin. These visits were always anticipated with eagerness by all, but even more so by Lesa as she returned to her childhood farmhouse on the scenic hillside overlooking the beautiful Lake Kegonsa.

As Lesa's father listened to our plan to begin our own business, preferably in the country, he said, "I think I know just the place you are looking for. We rent some farmland that has a vacant farmhouse and a new four-car garage on it that could be used as a shop."

We knew instantly as we walked around the beautiful, wooded farmland that this would be one adventurous spot for our family to continue to live and grow together. There was even a ready-built campfire pit just waiting for the first match to bring it to life. A phone call to the owner and we were packing and headed north. This 80 acre farm would definitely require some immediate exploring.

As soon as the major unloading was done, six little explorers raced to the woods and the barn to see what could be discovered. We all thanked God that night for allowing us to live in such a beautiful country setting. Every day was a new adventure with so much new territory to explore. Several pets joined the farm, assisting in various exploring expeditions.

One day, as Lesa was unpacking one of the remaining boxes, she found a piece of folded paper that aroused her curiosity. She smiled as she remembered the little game that she had played with the kids just before lunch one day back in Rochelle, and read through the list of dreams that had been recorded months before. She called each of the participants to come and share her discovery. They all looked eagerly over the dream list. Somehow, the man with the million dollar check must have misplaced our address or had car trouble or some other unexpected emergency, because he never arrived. But in one of God's many acts of kindness to our family He had given every wish they had listed and more besides.

This old farm was instantly the place for youth groups to come to sing around the campfire, roast marshmallows, cook out, go on hay rides, fill the yard with tents for campouts, or come just for the fun of exploring the woods. Four horses soon found their way to the pasture adding to the adventure. Dogs, cats, and a pet raccoon were added to the abundant blessings we knew had been provided for us by a kind and loving Father in heaven. One corner of the farm had been home for some Indians who had made their encampment in the woods near Lake Kegonsa many years earlier. This area required repeated exploration to locate arrowheads and other artifacts that might be discovered. For a group of ready made explorers, what better setting than a true-to-life Indian campground? A barn half full of hay with a loft provided the perfect place for forts to be built and many a leap in the hay with friends after school. Truly, God provided a wonderful place for our family to grow together.

Heidi, who was now almost 13 years old, decided she wanted to go and live with her mother in Idaho. It was a sad day for our patched together family the day Heidi drove down the driveway for the last time. The day Heidi left our home on the farm for the mountains of Idaho, we all experienced some of the fresh pain that is always a reality in every divorce and the consequent complications that follow. It was not a mystery to any of us why God says in His word, "I hate divorce." I am so thankful that He helped our family make the emotional adjustments necessary to move on and trust Him as we continued our journey with Him.

After enjoying several years on the farm, an unexpected development came along that drastically changed our lives. At a church potluck, I began talking to Ron Crary, a close friend with a wonderful spirit of adventure, and director of Country Life Restaurant in Madison, Wisconsin. When I say "spirit of adventure," I truly mean it. One book

Lord, If We Could Choose

could never contain all the exploits of Ron Crary and his family. Ron began to tell me about the newest adventure forthcoming in his life. A group in the Dominican Republic, interested in building a vegetarian restaurant, had contacted him. He shared some of the challenges and obstacles that would have to be worked through as we enjoyed the fellowship of a nice, potluck meal together.

After a few minutes, the thought occurred to him that recruiting some help might not be a bad idea. "Would you like to come along?" he asked. What a question to ask of another person that loved adventure.

In a few weeks, we were on a plane south bound for the Caribbean country of the Dominican Republic on the island of Hispaniola. It was late by the time we finished with customs and began the short commute along the palm-lined coast to Santo Domingo. A two story building across from the university district would be the site to be developed as the new restaurant. We fell asleep that night on the floor of this empty building amidst much scurrying and commotion of the creatures that also called this building home. It became a matter of frustration to us that these creatures slept in the day and played war games with the garbage all night.

Our team worked long hours into the night rebuilding and designing rooms, counters, and kitchen cupboards to be more effectively used for the new restaurant. As the time for our project was coming to a close, it became obvious that more help would be needed to make this project a reality. A small mission school in a very remote setting had also been started in conjunction with the restaurant. Many aspects of the project remained unfinished and would need to be completed before opening its doors as a school.

As I sat out on the steps one night watching and listening to all that was taking place across the street at the university, God spoke to me. I felt His presence around me as He said, "I want you to move here with your family to work for me." I said, "Lord, are You sure about this? I am not so sure Lesa will want to leave a farm in the country for all this poverty and sadness." The plane trip home was filled with mixed emotions as I tried to imagine how I would tell Lesa that I believed God was calling our family to the Dominican Republic as missionaries.

After the excitement of my homecoming had died down and each bed had the right number of occupants, I broke the news to Lesa. She

I Will Save You to Make You a Blessing

listened momentarily, though it was a rather brief moment, before informing me she didn't want to hear another word about it. Fortunately, I had learned at least one key communication skill in marriage for situations just such as this: don't say a word!

A real struggle started within Lesa as the same conviction began to settle on her. After several days of prayer and arguing with God, she finally opened her heart to God saying, "Alright God, if this is what You really want, I will go, but I have to know for sure that this is really You. I don't want to go to some faraway place filled with impossible challenges and blame Greg for everything that goes wrong. I have to know this is really You. Lord, I know if You are calling Greg, You are calling all of us. Please, make Your will clear as I present this project to the children. I will accept Your leading and look for Your providence in the attitude of our children."

Lesa gathered what she hoped would be a band of faithful supporters for the homeland cause around her as she presented the mission project. This would be her spreading of a "Gideon fleece." I knew the same marital principle and rule of appropriate times for speaking was still in force, so I wisely chose to listen silently.

The presentation began with, "We are considering a move to one of the most remote portions of planet Earth. In such places many challenges exist and are part of everyday life that we never experience here at home. Out in the remote portion of the country we would be living in there would be no plumbing. This would of course mean there would be no showers; all water would have to be carried up a steep hill from a little stream in pails; each of you would have to wash your own laundry, requiring long hours of scrubbing by hand. This would be a venture in faith, so there might not be any birthday presents, Christmas presents, or possibly food at times as we would never know when money would come."

I wondered if I could endure the insects, rats, bats, poverty and hardships that I heard being presented to this little band of would-be missionaries. All friendships with classmates and friends would soon be only a distant memory and would in all probability be an eternal loss; all the fun of the farm, all pets, everything that is pleasant in life, would be but a distant memory from the past, if such a venture ensued. Many such missionary families are never heard of again once they leave and

Lord, If We Could Choose

go to such far removed places as the one under consideration. With the fervor of a politician making his last campaign speech before an election, Lesa reminded them this would be the reality of their life, perhaps forever, if they were to agree to such a preposterous venture.

"Lord, I hope you can handle these odds," I thought as the presentation neared its conclusion. After the last gloomy prospect had been presented, it was time for the vote. In a state of disbelief, Lesa watched five hands quickly lift heavenward, affirming the mission endeavor followed by the chorus: "When do we leave?" Surely her impassioned presentation had not been understood; there must be some lacking clarity that needed to be added.

A fervent repeat of the presentation ensued; perhaps sufficient emphasis had been lacking at key points of the presentation. When the votes were re-tallied, the enthusiastic campaigner for the homeland cause was in a state of disbelief. The vote cast by show of hands revealed the same results in the second tally as the first. It was now evident that only God could have influenced such a landslide decision. (The remote possibility exists that portions of the above presentation to the future young missionaries might have been embellished for the purpose of story enhancement.)

One evening, as our departure drew near, Lesa sat on the porch contemplating what she would share at church the next day, as it would probably be her last opportunity before leaving for a new home far away. It was the cool of the evening with a gentle breeze rustling the leaves in the trees overhead. The evening sun added to the picturesque landscape with horses quietly grazing in the pasture. All at once the whole beautiful scene caused a feeling of lonesomeness to flood her soul. She hadn't left yet, but this scene didn't seem to belong to her anymore. "Lord," she said, "it won't be very long until I will be in another country faraway from here, wishing I could be seeing what I am seeing right now."

At that moment, she felt God come very close with a gentleness that she could almost touch. His voice held a warm smile as He recounted to her the memory of the way we came to call this farm our home. Memories washed over her as she thought of His gift of love to her in this country setting. He knew she would love everything about the place He had given her. In a very gentle voice she heard Him say, "I

I Will Save You to Make You a Blessing

have something better for you now." She knew that He hadn't meant a better place—one that she would like better than this one. She knew He was talking about a blessing, and that was what she wanted for her family more than anything else.

At that very moment, His love for her and how pleased He was with her choice to go where He desired surrounded her. She felt the assurance that her decision to follow God's plan had somehow brought honor and happiness to the heart of her Heavenly Father.

The day finally came when seven missionaries drove down the long driveway en route to the plane that would take them to their new home. As the plane floated far above the beautiful Caribbean below, five little faces pressed close to the small plane windows trying not to miss any of the adventure from such an exciting journey. As our plane banked, making a final approach to the runway, the same five little faces pressed close to windows in wonder at the landscape of their new home. The narrow strip of blacktop below that cut its way through thick, tropical plants did not look like the runway they had taken off from.

With our bags in hand, we walked across the runway in the hot tropical sun as an initiation to this new country. We were greeted by local organizers of the little mission project. A few suitcases and a few boxes didn't seem like much when it represented everything we had to start working in a new country. As we drove along the palm lined highway to Santo Domingo, our minds filled with all sorts of questions about what this new life would bring.

8
Our New Home

Challenges greeted us at every turn in this new land. The obvious hurdles such as none of us speaking Spanish (unless you call counting to ten speaking Spanish), the vast differences in culture, and being transportation-dependent in an extremely remote area, would have been sufficient, but since my last visit to this country the government had undergone some major difficulties.

The value of Dominican currency was being challenged by the international community. All shipments of grain had been halted. Shipments of gasoline, propane, and kerosene had been all but cut off, leaving long lines around city blocks with people standing holding empty cans, bottles, and jugs sometimes for days, just for a turn at the pump. This was definitely something we had never experienced before. People had to go to the bakery in the morning and stand in line until the afternoon for an opportunity to purchase a single loaf of bread.

The garbage companies either had no fuel for their trucks or were on strike, causing an unbelievable mess in a city of a million people. People were, for the most part, learning to just deal with the emergency. These added challenges did little to bring peace of mind to my missionary wife. We were told our container would be held up in customs for a few more days (which turned out to be a year).

After waiting for a few days in Santo Domingo at the partially completed restaurant, we decided to go to the little mission school in the country and begin our work. We loaded our suitcases and personal belongings into a small pickup and began the two hour journey into the inland. It was the rainy season in the tropics, and that meant rains like

I Will Save You to Make You a Blessing

we had never seen before. Without any type of canopy for the little truck, we just headed down the road, ladies in front and suitcases and men in the back. The last seven miles to the school proved to us why the location was classified as remote. Sugar cane tractors and trailers caused large sink holes, ruts, and muddy lakes in the road during the rainy season that were a cause for concern even for four-wheel-drive vehicles. It was all we could do to plow our way through with our little pickup which was loaded beyond capacity.

It was dark when we arrived at our new home. A partially completed little three bedroom block house, minus a back door, awaited us for occupancy. The handful of students and staff living at the school had been using this house as a temporary cafeteria for the past several months. A few old roots and vegetables were stacked in the back corner near the opening where the door should have been. A sheet of plywood supported by stacks of concrete blocks would be our new dining room table. The house was dark as we arrived with only a dim, smoky, flickering lamp burning diesel fuel on the table. The flickering of this dim flame through the smoky, glass chimney caused an eerie, shadowy dance on the walls as we began to carry our things from the rainy outside to the inside of our new home. Our boxes and suitcases were more than a little damp from the long ride in the back of the pickup, as were the menfolk.

Our chauffeur was anxious to leave as he still had to negotiate a return trip. As soon as the last box was removed from the truck, he was gone. We had no transportation, we couldn't speak Spanish, and we were seven miles from the closest electricity or telephone. It appeared Lesa's prophecy was more truth than fiction. We knew God had brought us here, and He would help us with all the incredible challenges that were already greeting us at every turn.

Lesa located a flashlight and began to explore her new abode. As the flashlight illuminated the walls and corners of the floors, large spiders the size of a man's hand created a wallpaper pattern all around the rooms. The spiders seemed totally unconcerned and unafraid of people. Evidently, human spider-killers like Lesa had never crossed their path before. This haven of refuge for spiders was about to encounter an all-out assault by a very determined foreign task force. Lesa and her company of young female assailants took off their flip-flops and began a

Our New Home

vigorous campaign to establish territorial rights. In just seconds our little house sounded like an auditorium full of people applauding a wonderful performance as the flip-flops contacted the wall in a rapid, machine-gun fire manner. In just minutes there were piles of spiders lying on the floor of each room. From that moment on all such creatures must enter this newly established domain at great risk to the longevity of their lives.

Youth size bunk beds were the only furnishings to be found in the house. Each had some old mosquito netting with holes large enough to render the whole piece of cloth useless unless, one might be trying to keep falling beach balls from landing on their heads while sleeping. In the darkness with flickering shadows and moving creatures, some of the new residents felt like they had stepped directly into a scene of some forgotten, scary movie. Mosquitoes were in such abundance that the air was literally filled with a singing sound as clouds of mosquitoes conversed concerning the meal that would soon be theirs when the newcomers lay down to attempt to sleep. The little lamp on the table was like an invitation to come in and begin the selection of which new-comer each mosquito might like to initiate to the jungle.

As we stared around the room, we noticed that bats had joined the party in response to the clouds of singing mosquitoes. Without a door on the back of the house, or any screens on the windows, and the entire area between the top of the wall and the tin roof open, any attempt to keep creatures that normally would not share habitation with humans, on the outside, appeared to be futile. We would just have to do the best we could. We bedded down in what seemed more like a jungle inside than it was outside. I suppose many readers have warm, cuddly feelings just about now and would give anything for a chance to trade places with one of those about to bed down on one of the 24-inch wide youth cots with springs sagging halfway to the floor. If you are one of these covetous ones, you will just have to mentally experience this night along with us, since it would be impossible to return in time.

It wasn't long after the lamp went out that we discovered that the rats had a regular freeway route through the house. The scamper of all those running feet, and the squeals and shrieks that rats make as they tussle for the same morsel, did not do a great deal to comfort and reassure most of the wary newcomers. It was unfortunate that we missed the sound of snakes capturing and eating rats that night. We were told

I Will Save You to Make You a Blessing

later that this home had been the site for such feasts in the past. I don't know why, but it seems like it would have added one more interesting dimension to our first night. Lesa and I were so thankful that, in spite of all that was going on, we soon heard restful breathing sounds coming from the other cots around us.

Lesa was in a top cot above me, not even close to closing her eyes in sleep. I think that I had forgotten to tell her sleep is impossible when the human body is in a stiff-as-a-board posture.

Almost as soon as we heard the restful breathing sounds coming from the beds of our young missionaries across the room, we felt the entrance of an unwanted presence. We could sense that this spiritual presence of darkness would like to encourage us to return home. Many of the feelings and sensations of past encounters returned and surrounded us. In the darkness Lesa called out to me, "Greg something is crawling all over the net right around my face, making strange slurping and gurgling sounds!" It was too dark to make out what was crawling around inches from her head but the moving, swaying net, combined with this slurping, gurgling noise, provided sufficient evidence that there was in fact something crawling around up there. Spirits of darkness continued to surround us with their presence hour after hour. Lesa literally thought the pounding in her heart was going to cause heart failure at any moment.

If you think a 24-inch cot is small for one, we soon proved that it is even smaller when two are occupying the space. Two persons in one such cot did very little to take the droop out of the already tired and sagging springs that were insufficient to support a single inmate, let alone two.

It was sometime in the early morning hours that our spiritual visitors decided it was time for the grand finale. A massive crash, that sounded like a huge boulder had fallen out of the sky landing on the tin roofing directly above our heads, caused both of us to freeze in place. These spirits let us know throughout the night that we were not welcome here. Even though it was a long and wearisome night, we knew our God had not left us to fight His battles in our strength.

Morning finally came to some blurry, red-eyed newcomers. Lesa and I carefully examined the roofing to see how large the dent might be from the enormous crash during the night, but to our amazement there

Our New Home

was not even a ripple in it. No foreign objects lay close by that could have created such an explosive sound either. It was clear the devil was trying to scare us home before we could even start a work for God in a countryside filled with people that have practiced voodoo for decades.

The second discovery of the morning came as we prepared to sweep up all the spider piles; not even the leg of one spider could be found. Armies of ants had completely cleaned the floor and were probably calling a special holiday feast with more dead spider meat than they had ever seen in their lives. We were all covered with insect bites. Rachel won the contest though, with over two hundred fifty mosquito bites that looked like they were stacked one on top of the other in many places.

Closing in the house took top priority, just as soon as a trip to a hardware store could be arranged. A sheet of plywood was purchased with some foam rubber that would be our new bed. New netting surrounded each bed. The luxury of a back door soon found its way to the gaping hole in the wall at the back of the house. We were sure that things would be better now that the house was sealed from the outside intruders. One major problem remained: a large family of rats had been trapped in the house with no way to escape.

One night one of these trapped adventurers decided the foam we were sleeping on would be fun to crawl under. We awoke with a moving lump under the foam, starting at our feet, moving upward to our heads. We began to pound frantically from the top side of the foam as close as we could to the lump underneath. Like a frightened missile this rat shot up into our bed and out through the net into less dangerous territory. (Lesa was very slow to acquire any tolerance or sympathy for rodent visitors in her bed! Some things are more difficult to learn than others, I guess.) Small details like this would from time to time make our room more like a rodent circus than a bedroom. Did you know that rats can run sideways on a concrete wall? In a few weeks, with numerous techniques, we had the inside of our house to ourselves.

Jungle home school commenced, and we began to focus on the purpose for which we had come to this new country. Gardens were planted, roads were repaired, and work started on some of the buildings. We prayed that God could make a difference in this little spot on planet Earth through a family that loved Him and wanted to share His

I Will Save You to Make You a Blessing

loving kindness with those around them.

I would like to encourage you if you are facing some fearful situation in your life right now. The devil desires to use fear as a powerful immobilizer in every Christian's life. We must constantly remind ourselves of the victory gained at Calvary and take courage in the One who so freely offers His victory to you and me. Perhaps you have chosen to memorize a scripture mentioned earlier in this book: "For I have not given you the spirit of timidity but of power and love and self control" (2 Timothy 1:7). Listen for God's voice; He will speak these words to you.

Do you know someone who is serving as a missionary? You may never know the depths of the challenges that are everyday life for them, but you can make an important difference to their ministry. Why don't you stop and pray for them right now? Your prayers will give them some much-needed courage when struggles come their way. Your faithfulness in prayer can change the entire atmosphere they are working in. Any missionary will tell you; praying people at home make all the difference in the world.

9
Concrete Trouble

With so many projects needing attention it was hard to know where to begin. We definitely needed some help. Just before leaving our home in Wisconsin, we called a young man named Fred Flint. Fred had mechanical skills as well as some agricultural experience and a deep love for the Lord. All of us felt encouraged when this energetic young man arrived to help in our project.

Fred instantly began to plant gardens and make necessary repairs on the many pieces of equipment that had been resting in an inoperative state. We were also blessed with the musical talents his voice and trumpet provided, changing the whole atmosphere of our little mission as hymns of praise filled the air. Fred was definitely an answer to prayer.

My sister, Sherry, was an RN working as a visiting nurse in Madison, Wisconsin. She thought perhaps it wouldn't be so bad to take a break from all the stress of nursing and exchange it for the challenges of mission life. The jungle home school instantly doubled in its staff and administration as Sherry joined Lesa in the teaching ranks. The pupils were glad for the extra tutoring as well. Sherry also set out to broaden the menu. This was no small challenge. With very few ingredients, and almost none of those familiar to us, the experiments began. All who helped with food preparation would agree that most of what took place in the kitchen resembled creation week—making something from nothing. All of us were encouraged to see the way God was teaching us to work as a team. We learned to appreciate the importance and value of each person who was contributing to make this mission project a success.

I Will Save You to Make You a Blessing

The restaurant project in the city had been progressing slowly with many challenges of its own. One project in particular needed our attention before the customers could safely approach the entrance of the building. The concrete parking area between the steps and the road in front of the restaurant was cracked and broken, making it difficult to negotiate in many places. We received a gift in the mail from friends at home that would be just enough to replace the broken concrete. Two young students assured me of their expertise and experience in concrete construction; they became the designated craftsman who would enable the project to flow along smoothly. With a few tools we set out for the city. It was apparent that my ready craftsmen were eager to demonstrate their skills on this special project.

It was not easy work removing a concrete slab without the aid of the equipment and power tools we would have used at home, but we managed to make progress with mauls, shovels, and picks. At the end of a long, hot, sweaty day, the slab was gone and a very large pile of concrete lay at the edge of the street. The next day we arranged for a ready mix truck to deliver the necessary cement. I knew it would be a challenge to keep ahead of a hot tropical sun, which would act as a catalyst, perhaps hastening the setting process more rapidly than desired.

While we were waiting for the ready mix truck to arrive, we reviewed our individual roles as cement finishers to ensure the smooth success of our slab-to-be. My young craftsmen wore broad smiles on their faces as they leaned on their shovels, calmly waiting for our truck. It soon arrived with our concrete, and we began to pour the first section of our slab. Almost immediately, I realized our communication had broken down. My helpers could be observed still leaning on their shovels with the same broad, beaming smiles they were wearing while we waited.

"Juan, Ramon, come on! We are going to have to hurry. This concrete will not wait in this hot sun," I pleaded. I frantically tried to hasten the strike-off process so we could proceed to the finishing before it was too late. I looked again to my reinforcements. It was impossible to notice or measure any increase in vigor. It didn't seem like they were attacking their portion of the concrete. Leaning on their shovels and rakes, they appeared to be quite content to watch me work like a madman. Why was I so uptight? These two helpers doodled and dabbed

Concrete Trouble

at the concrete, totally relaxed with the same beaming smiles.

By the time the truck pulled away and we were able to start the finishing process, the concrete had already become very stiff and hard to manage. The same broad smiles combined with the same lack of vigor were repeated in the finishing process. They watched as I scrubbed frantically like a power trowel running at full throttle. Seven gallons of sweat and ten blisters later, our project was completed. It was not perfect by any means, but considering the circumstances, it turned out pretty well. Isn't it amazing what can be accomplished when we all work together as a team!

A few days later, Juan and Fred accompanied me back to the city to remove the mountain of broken pieces of concrete that remained piled high at the street. In the absence of a dump truck, we used the Mitsubishi Montero from the mission, towing a large homemade trailer to haul away the concrete. We inquired where there might be some kind of landfill or site for dumping the old concrete. No one knew of such a place. The answer was pretty much the same from everyone: find a place where others have been dumping broken block and concrete and add to the pile.

As we were loading the trailer, I remembered seeing several such sites along the edge of the coastal highway. The large trailer was piled high and loaded beyond capacity as we pulled away from the curb. We traveled the three or four blocks to the highway along the ocean and began our search for a site to unload our goods. The concrete was not our only problem, however; our homemade trailer was a donation from the United States and had no manufacturer's identification tag with the necessary numbers required for a license plate. We had attempted to acquire a license plate on more than one occasion, going from one government office to another without success.

The coastal highway quite often had police checkpoints to monitor proper licenses, insurance papers, or any other legal inconsistency. We held our breath, hoping today would not be a day for traffic checks. A mile or two down the road we spotted several tall mounds of broken concrete. It was evident that several large dump trucks had unloaded here some time earlier. We backed up to one of the piles and began adding our concrete to the pile. We had just begun when a car pulled alongside and the driver said, "You better not unload that there, or you

I Will Save You to Make You a Blessing

will be arrested." We asked him where we could find a place to unload, but he knew of no such place. We pulled back onto the coastal highway and continued our search.

Our fears of a roadblock became a reality just a couple miles down the road. The officer inspected our papers and licenses then asked us where the license plate was for the trailer. Juan came to the rescue explaining that we were missionaries and the difficulty we had encountered trying to acquire the missing license plate. After some time, the expression on the officer's face softened; he smiled and said we could go. We breathed a thank you to the Lord as it was almost unheard of to escape such a predicament without significant funds exchanging hands. "Officer, perhaps you can help us with the correct location to unload this concrete," I said.

He thought for a moment and said, "I really don't know for sure, but why don't you find a pile along the road and just add yours to it."

We smiled and drove away—this was our day. Sure enough, in another couple miles we spotted just such a site. Numerous piles of broken concrete and blocks were piled high from what appeared to have been random dumping by some very large trucks. Once again we backed up to a large pile and began to throw off the unwanted concrete. After a lot of hard, sweaty work, our mountain of concrete was almost gone.

Just as we prepared to throw one of the few remaining pieces from the trailer, the sound of yelling, screaming, and pounding feet halted all unloading progress. From across the highway, a young soldier came running and waving his arms, yelling at the top of his lungs. We waited for his approach to discover the reason for the war cry that he probably had learned in basic training for situations where national security had been threatened by an all-out attack from an invasion force taking over the island. We knew he meant business as he approached with his World War II machine gun pointed directly at us. He was so excited, and my Spanish was still so limited, that I turned to Juan and asked, "What is all this about?"

Juan was visibly shaken as he relayed the fact that we were under arrest for dumping on government property. Speaking through my trembling interpreter, I tried to explain the instructions we had just received from the police only a couple miles down the road. Every attempt to clarify our position only seemed to make our captor all the more determined. He was very young, and it seemed that we might be the first actual criminals he had ever apprehended. It became increasingly clear that he was not about to let us slip through his fingers. He looked to be about twenty and rather new to his post, with full fatigues and all. He was beginning to appear rather irritated with the lack of respect he was getting from his newly apprehended criminals, who seemed to be stalling.

I asked Juan, "What does he want us to do?"

He said, "He is taking us to headquarters in the capital."

I tried to reason with him, offering to reload all the concrete and haul it away. Now he was serious at the thought of losing his criminal trophies! His finger moved closer to the trigger and pointing the barrel at me said, "Get in the jeep." I stood looking at the eighth-inch between his finger and an engaged trigger; I looked at the long row of machine gun bullets and wondered what to do next. I hadn't had much practice in situations with machine guns, so I just decided to do whatever he asked.

The whole idea seemed so absurd, but we loaded into the Montero and headed for Santo Domingo. Juan had heard far too many stories about the prison system in his country to do anything but turn white as we made our way back up the highway to the city. Fred wasn't feeling that comfortable with the whole idea of being under arrest and heading to a government compound either. We prayed in silence as this serious young soldier kept the gun barrel pointed in my direction while we traveled the short distance back to Santo Domingo. I discovered that machine gun bullets look a lot bigger while being viewed from close proximity.

Following the instructions of the one riding shotgun, (I guess "machine gun" would be more appropriate in this case), we continued up one of the main streets until we saw a two-story concrete compound that took up a large portion of a city block. On one corner of the compound, a large archway provided the only opening to the inner court. The one giving the directions motioned us into the large archway guarded by other soldiers equally as serious about their responsibilities. We were stopped momentarily as the soldiers communicated concerning their captives. Offices and holding cells were built into the two-story, concrete

I Will Save You to Make You a Blessing

wall that lined the perimeter of the giant courtyard. Truly, the whole structure looked very imposing in its setting. It seemed to fit the colonial setting in Santo Domingo with numerous structures dating back to the days of Columbus.

Armed soldiers were everywhere. Soldiers of every rank moved busily about their business. We were instructed to pull just inside the courtyard, Montero, trailer and all. The attending soldiers began a brief search for the colonel as the commanding officer to preside over our case. We were about to be brought to trial here and now in this open courtyard. After a moment or two, the colonel was located sitting at a large desk talking to another officer in the far corner of the courtyard. We pulled to one side of the courtyard and parked. We began walking toward the large desk in the courtyard with our proud escort walking just behind us. He was dead serious about preventing our escape even after entering this massive, concrete fortress. It appeared that he was studying our every move lest we should decide to fight our way through the scores of armed soldiers and scale the two story concrete wall. Studying the technique of our captor, one would think he was single-handedly bringing to justice three escaped convicts from death row.

Needless to say, our little parade instantly dominated the attention of every soldier and officer. As our company came to a halt in front of a large desk with two well decorated officers seated behind, we learned that truly this was our day—the colonel would not hear our case after all as he was deferring it to the visiting general seated next to him. With the general presiding and the show that had just taken place, the officers began to pour over to this corner of the courtyard, as if a Broadway play was about to open. I listened with limited understanding to the charges as they were being relayed to the listening general. It became quite clear that this hearing would not be without an audience as more and more soldiers kept coming from who knows where. All at once, we were surrounded by soldiers of every rank, all desiring to be a part of this festive occasion. Now instead of a dozen or so witnesses, our little party filled one whole portion of the courtyard. My student translator was so terrified he had become totally mute. No sounds could be heard coming from Fred that might be considered contributions for our liberation or support for our cause, either. My Spanish was very limited, but I did know the difference between the word for garbage and concrete.

Concrete Trouble

This young soldier continued to press his case before this grand tribunal stating that he had caught us throwing out a trailer-load of garbage along the highway.

Silently, I prayed, asking for the Lord to somehow bring some sanity to this whole ordeal that seemed to me to be slightly out of proportion. Just then, another soldier stepped out of the crowd and made an attempt to translate for me, allowing me to make at least a partial explanation. The general appeared to be enjoying the honor and attention this festive event was providing him. After several charges and the following rebuttals, combined with several periods of attempted clarification, the general appeared to have reached a verdict.

In full authority, the general said, "I will dismiss your incarceration; all three of you are free to go, but I am keeping your Montero and trailer as government property."

"Sir," I said, "I cannot agree to your terms. You may not have our Montero." I began to explain that an entire mission school depended on this Montero as its only means of transportation.

Every eye was on the general now to see what he would do with these three criminals who had refused to accept his terms. He said, "I am sorry. You will have to leave the vehicle here, but you are free to go."

"Sir," I said, "I cannot go without this Montero. It's simply out of the question; our mission is totally dependent on it."

Now he appeared to be a little flustered as he tried to decide what to do and still appear to be the one in control. After a moment of silence he said, "Okay, you can take your Montero, but the trailer stays. You are free to go."

"Sir," I said, "I cannot accept your terms. Our school is equally dependent on this trailer to transport all our supplies to its remote location." He looked stern as he said, "The trailer stays!"

"Sir, I simply cannot leave without this trailer. That's all there is to it."

A moment of silence hung in the air for what seemed like an eternity with all eyes on the general, awaiting his final decision. Finally, with what appeared to be a combination of frustration, embarrassment, and anger he said, "Okay, take the Montero and trailer, but you must go back and pick up every piece of concrete that you discarded."

I am sure the general didn't mean to leave us with a wrong impression, but I think that he would not welcome or encourage our

I Will Save You to Make You a Blessing

enlistment in his armed forces. I suppose good soldiers are difficult to find in every country. I'm not really sure what caused me to sense his displeasure. Maybe it was the expresssion on his face or the look in his eye, but something made me feel that he was just as glad to see us leave as we were to exit this very imposing, concrete compound. We hadn't in any way intended to be disrespectful, it was just that his previous suggestions would have been a great hindrance to the cause of God.

"Thank you, sir," I said as I turned and walked toward the Montero. I didn't discuss it with him any further, but I was thinking: wasn't the option of picking up the concrete and reloading it into the trailer the same suggestion we had made at the beginning of this whole ordeal some time ago?

As I walked across the vast courtyard returning to the waiting Montero and trailer, I sensed the presence of God come very close as I heard Him say, "Some day soon my people will testify before kings and governors in My name." I was reminded that we do not need to prepare what we will say at such a moment, we only need to stay close to the One who will tell us what to say.

The concrete was not any lighter when we were reloading it than it was any of the other times we had handled it, but we had a song in our hearts as we realized that the enemy's plans to halt God's work had been overruled.

Perhaps the enemy is causing you to feel very defeated in some area of your life right now. Perhaps it feels like your case has outrageous odds stacked against it. The devil may be a masterful general plotting your ruin and destruction, but he is nothing when confronted with the Captain of the Lord of Hosts. Not once has Our Captain ever been strategically challenged when faced with even the most masterful plans of his opposing general. I want to assure you that our Captain is well able to handle your case in every particular. He invites you to watch Him fight on your behalf. Listen as He personally speaks to you. "Fear ye not, stand still, and see the salvation of the LORD, which he will show to you today: for the Egyptians whom ye have seen today, ye shall see them again no more for ever. The LORD shall fight for you, and ye shall hold your peace" (Exodus 14:13-14).

10
Sharing the Gospel

God's little mission school slowly began to take shape. The gardens began to look beautiful as well as adding some much-needed variety to our diets. Beautiful pineapple plants formed long rows, promising tropical fruit salads in the not-too-distant future. Orange trees were beginning to look more like trees than bushes. Many of the buildings had undergone improvements and finishing touches as funds had become available. Several gardens with tropical plants and rocks were added to the landscape. The leaves of the banana plants glistened in the sunlight and rustled in the afternoon breezes.

A new generator provided periods of electricity, and a new well meant plenty of fresh water. We continued to pray that God would make this mission a shining light in the darkness of a remote area that was steeped in voodoo. We prayed for the privilege of sharing Jesus with the many neighbors around us who had grown up with these practices of darkness and superstition. We were all very thankful when He answered our prayers by sending us an evangelist from Mexico.

David, Virginia, Moses, and Karen Cruz each contributed significantly as a family ministry team dedicated to the task of sharing the gospel. We began to see almost immediately that God was providing all sorts of new possibilities for our school. Young people from any of the surrounding churches who wished to increase their knowledge of the Bible, as well as improving skills necessary for sharing the gospel more effectively, were invited to come and enroll in a field school for evangelism. Soon students and teacher could be seen hiking the trails with their Bibles, visiting and sharing with anyone who had a spiritual interest.

I Will Save You to Make You a Blessing

Every Friday night a worship service was planned with special music, stories, songs for the children, and sharing from the Word of God. The people started to pack our little chapel each Friday evening, joining in the singing and listening intently to the preaching of the Word. Many walked for long distances in the twilight to reach the worships and then returned in the darkness without even a flashlight. Truly, a new light was shining in this little spot on planet Earth which had been darkened by centuries of spiritual darkness.

David and the students began to plan for a series of meetings in a nearby town that would allow others to hear the good news. Several afternoons a week the students accompanied David to this town, walking up and down the streets simply asking people if they would like to study the Bible or if they would be interested in prayer for some specific need that might be weighing heavily on their heart. After a few weeks, the students returned from the little town with big smiles on their faces saying, "People are beginning to call to us from their yards, saying, 'Come over to my house and study with me.'" It was evident that God was blessing His little band of workers.

One day David came back from a visit with a group of people living in a very remote location, requesting all at the mission to accompany him on his next visit. He knew we would want to help this group of very needy people he had just discovered. The ladies prepared food and clothing to share with David's new-found friends from supplies that had been donated for those in most desperate need. We went as far as the road could take our Montero and passenger-cargo trailer, parked, and began our hike to the remote clearing these people called home. We all had to wade across a swift, little river which meant forming a human chain to prevent any of the smaller missionaries from being swept away by the current. "What must it be like to grow up in a place so far removed from civilization?" I thought as we climbed the bank of the river on the other side and continued our hike, dripping as we went along. Soon we came to a clearing with three or four very crude huts. The reality of growing up in such a far removed place seemed to strike all of us at once as we gazed at children perhaps ten or eleven years of age who apparently had never owned clothing of any kind. We sang some songs and shared the gifts that had been prepared for them. The big, beautiful smiles made it quite clear that even the smallest items

Sharing the Gospel

were very much appreciated. We couldn't help remembering the abundances of our families and friends at home, wishing there was a way to share some of what we throw away in our land of plenty.

David shared a message of hope and courage from God's Word and offered a short prayer before we returned by the path on which we had come. In every encounter with the destitute and hopeless, we couldn't help wishing that our gift wasn't so small and inadequate compared with the overwhelming needs that haunted us on every side. There are so many places on this planet that have been darkened with the curse of sin that it makes your heart long for the day that all will be made new and such poverty, hunger, and disease will be forever gone.

Many adventures could be told of the little motorcycle that our mission school used for transportation and sharing the gospel in our remote location. The many miles of use over the rough and rugged terrain left our little motorcycle in a much less than new condition. With many a prayer the motorcycle, piloted by David with a student seated behind, set out for visits in the country to share the gospel with neighbors in remote areas.

Returning from one such afternoon visit, David called us to come and hear the latest miracle that God had used to further the gospel and reach a family for His kingdom. David and a student evangelist were making their way to the nearest village for a Bible study with a family eager to learn more of the story of Jesus. They were about half way to the village when the motorcycle that had been running smoothly down the road came to an unexpected stop. The motor just died without warning, causing them to coast to a stop. They tried for some time to restart the motor, but without success.

Looking around for someone who might be able to assist them, they realized they had come to a stop almost directly in front of a little house right next to the road. They pushed the motorcycle up the path leading into the front yard and walked up to the door, hoping to find a solution to their dilemma. They were greeted warmly by the lady inside as they shared their plight with her. When she learned that David was an evangelist and the young man with him was a student Bible worker, she invited them to share God's word with her and her family. As the study proceeded, it was plain to see that God had arranged for this divine appointment with these honest seekers for truth.

I Will Save You to Make You a Blessing

After a lengthy study and many questions, the family eagerly invited the stranded evangelists to return soon that they might learn more from God's word. As he walked back to the waiting motorcycle, David's heart was overflowing with praise to God at His providence in leading them to the doorstep of people honest of heart and eager to join the family of God. There seemed to be no other option than to take turns pushing the motorcycle the several miles back to the mission school. The thought of pushing this motorcycle up and down hills in the heat of the tropical sun, as well as all the deep mud holes and ponds that occupied most of the space that should have been road, provided less than an inviting prospect. Waving goodbye, they wheeled their way back out into the little, country road.

David decided to try one last time to start the stalled motorcycle before beginning the long push back to the school. With a prayer and a kick on the starter, the engine came to life. The motor purred all the way back without even a sputter. It was no small wonder David was beaming as he shared with us the power of a God who proved once again that He was in charge and well able to manage the sharing of His message of love with the lost and lonely on planet Earth.

Several return visits to the little family along the road followed, resulting in a complete surrender of their lives to the new friend they had found in Jesus and a decision to follow the Lord all the way in baptism. This little family has continued to hold fast their commitment to the Lord Jesus, and they are still rejoicing in Him today.

David soon learned of another family some distance from our little mission school that desired a visit. He asked me if I would drive him on the motorcycle as the rainy season that was well under way presented a whole new set of challenges. Our little road-path-ditch was also shared by the sugar cane tractors and trailers harvesting and hauling the cane to market. The large four-wheel drive tractors and trailers left deep ruts in the knee deep mud that occupied the majority of the road we needed to negotiate in order to reach this little family.

Together we mounted the trusty motorcycle and began the adventure of negotiating all the little side paths that skirted the deepest of the ponds and mud holes that made up many miles of the road that we had to pass to reach the main road. We sensed the presence of angels guiding us along many a journey to reach those desiring to learn of

Sharing the Gospel

Jesus. Slowly, we wound our way around the little paths along the road to reach the waiting family. We praised the Lord as we successfully negotiated the last little roadside pathway and turned into the little driveway of a very impoverished one-room home.

As we visited and shared the good news with these new members of God's family, my heart went out to the young mother and father, surrounded by small children and holding a little bundle containing their newest addition to a family, that already had all the signs of hopelessness. As far as I could see, this young mother had absolutely nothing within her barren home that would provide for the needs of her family. The small river that bordered their backyard created a perfect environment for the reproduction of the thick clouds of mosquitoes that were swarming us in the twilight. Once again our hearts ached for the members of God's family who had to suffer through such a miserable existence day after day without the hope of anything better to come. It was not hard to interest these dear people in a heaven without all the pain and suffering that they faced day after day.

The sun had quietly slipped over the horizon as we finished sharing pictures of a loving God who sent His Son on a wonderful rescue mission that included this little family. As we told them goodbye, we realized our return journey would be much more difficult with just the small beam of light from the headlight of our motorcycle to negotiate the narrow paths that crossed back and forth across the road in and around the deep mud holes. David and I climbed back on the motorcycle and started the engine, preparing to leave for the mission. Reaching for the light switch, I turned it to the ON position, but nothing happened. I turned it back and forth from the ON to OFF position several times without a flicker of light. We were in total darkness on a moonless and cloudy night without even the twinkle of a star from the blackened sky above.

Many sitting comfortably at home have little idea what darkness feels like without any form of light. Almost instantly, even the shadows disappear on moonless nights, making it impossible to see an object directly in front of you. Those who have gone down in caves and had the lights shut off will know the feeling I am trying to describe. Negotiating the road below us would be a total impossibility if we could not even see our hand extended in front of us.

I Will Save You to Make You a Blessing

We sat there in the darkness miles from home with an impossible terrain to negotiate, wondering how God would ever get us home in this incredible blackness. We prayed silently as we inched slowly forward in the direction we hoped was home. Without the aid of our eyes the only way to negotiate the road was by feel. Let me assure you that neither one of us had any experience riding a motorcycle using the Braille technique for navigation.

With my feet sliding along the uneven surface of the road and slightly extended outward feeling for grass, trees, rocks or anything that would indicate the edge of the road, we inched forward. The only way home would be directly through each of the mud holes we had so carefully skirted just a few hours earlier. Without a headlight, negotiating the pathways along the side of the road would be out of the question.

All too soon the reality of the muddy road greeted my shoes, socks, legs, and pants. Inching forward, we felt the motorcycle descending into one of the giant mud ponds that dominated most of the roadway. It was not really all that exciting to feel first my shoes and socks fill with mud and then a wet, oozy sensation climbing up my legs, causing my pants to feel like they had been pasted to my legs with a giant mud poultice. We slid from side to side from hidden rocks, tractor ruts, and other uneven terrain hidden far beneath the surface of mud. As we neared the far end of our first muddy hole in the road and began to climb back up to higher ground, the mud became thicker, requiring more power to plow our way through. Quickly accelerating to avoid stalling splattered the cool wet substance that engulfed our feet and legs onto our backs and heads from the airborne mud missiles caused by our spinning tire.

We felt a real sense of victory as we cleared the edge of the hole with our back tire and continue into the blackness feeling our way along. It was comforting to know that we had successfully crossed the first of the ten thousand such holes positioned between us and our homeward destination. (I don't think anyone actually counted each hole, so it seemed like an appropriate measure to approximate, plus or minus a few thousand.)

We inched our way through the darkness from side to side in the road. As our feet encountered one edge of the road, we would turn slightly the other way until we could feel the edge at the other side. We

Sharing the Gospel

had a little over eight kilometers to cover in this tedious manner. On more than one occasion we felt ourselves slide completely sideways, almost certain to fall over in the mud, only to feel the motorcycle stabilize and resume its course. It really is not possible to describe the reality of angels literally holding us up as we slipped and felt ourselves tipping over in the darkness only to be held upright in a moment of helplessness. It is a wonderful feeling to know that God has commissioned heavenly angels to protect and keep us in times of need. We were very aware of the fact that if we ever tipped over we could be seriously injured and stranded miles from nowhere with no one to help. God did not just send angels to Daniel in the lion's den and then discontinue His love and care for all that would follow; His watchful eye is ever focused upon you and me as well.

Time seemed to stand still as we inched our way back in the darkness. We knew we would have to cross a narrow bridge over a small stream as we neared the little mission. On either side were steep rocky banks that could be very dangerous if we missed the narrow bridge and plunged over the edge. We held our breath as we approached the area that we believed must be close to this little bridge. Soon we could hear the sound of the stream as the water rushed over the rocks below. We remembered well that the road made a sharp turn to the left just before the bridge. How would we ever negotiate the sharp turn in the road and still manage to end up finding the center of the bridge rather than plunging over one edge or the other?

The words "moving forward in blind faith" took on a whole new meaning as we felt ourselves moving forward in total blindness, approaching the turn in the road leading to the bridge. We praised the Lord as we went gliding across the narrow expanse, never once even touching the concrete edge on either side of the bridge. How thankful we were that we had the ministry of angels—heavenly beings that delight to care for God's children—to guide us back to the mission that night. It was very late when two exhausted missionaries made their entrance to the little mission, praising God for His wonderful guidance and watchful care.

The enemy of light and the prince of darkness was not about to allow people to be freed from his grasp without a fight. The priest in this area started to feel threatened by all the activity that was taking place

I Will Save You to Make You a Blessing

both in the country and in "his" town. He began an active campaign, attempting to counteract or undo anything we did to share the gospel. His biggest weapon seemed to be intimidation. Everyone in the entire region feared his displeasure.

The Montero began to experience mechanical problems that made the visits to town much more difficult. When transportation from a vehicle with four wheels was not available, David would climb back on the little motorcycle and continue his visits on two wheels.

Our hearts were saddened as yet another of the attacks was directed at one of the students enrolled in the lay ministry program. It filled us with sadness to watch this brave young student became very ill with all the symptoms of AIDS, making it necessary for him to return to his home. We were reminded that our warfare was not against flesh and blood but against spiritual forces in heavenly places.

The setbacks did not deter either evangelist or students. Arrangements were made for evangelistic meetings to begin just after the Christmas and New Year holidays. We were all ready for a little break and for some seasonal relaxation before beginning the meetings that are always exhausting and rewarding at the same time. With farewells and seasonal salutations, the students returned to their homes for a few weeks of holiday festivities with their families.

11
Life-Saving Mosquitoes

Everyone was ready for a little rest and all the joy and encouragement that the Christmas holiday always brings. Arrangements were made for our whole group to stay at a campground located directly on the Atlantic coast for a week of fun in the sun and surf. This would require some interesting travel arrangements with six adults, five teenagers and David's two younger children.

We had only the five-passenger Montero and the homemade trailer that had narrowly escaped confinement in a military prison. We constructed a canopy as a cover for the trailer, wrapping a blue plastic tarp over the top for waterproofing. With these new creations we now had transportation to accommodate our entire force.

At home people would have thought we were a float in a parade, but we weren't really that out of the ordinary where people carry beds on little motorcycles and small pickups carry twenty or thirty passengers. After loading enough sleeping bags and blankets, clothes, food, and water for thirteen, I am sure that we would have become an even more interesting entry in some exotic parade.

Just before leaving for our vacation, the Montero let us know it was getting very tired and in need of some repair. It started overheating every time we went even a short distance. The thought of starting out on a six hour journey across a mountain range hours from mechanical assistance would not have even entered our minds at home. This would be our only opportunity for a vacation, and everyone was willing to risk the possible delays that would no doubt become more and more

I Will Save You to Make You a Blessing

frequent as the problem with the head gasket would no doubt grow worse and worse. With all final votes cast to proceed, the loading was completed, and we were off. Did I forget to mention the surf board tied on or stuck in somewhere? We were ready for the beach!

All went well, or at least as we expected. There were frequent stops along the way for engine cooling, but that was ok, We were on vacation. After a few extra hours of travel, we arrived at the beautiful campground on the Atlantic Ocean.

As we pulled up next to the group lodge, we noticed another group of young missionaries that appeared to already be using the campsite. I walked over to greet this other group who were also obviously visitor missionaries to this country. To my surprise, I came face to face with Gary Burns, my cousin, a youth pastor from Michigan. Neither of us had any idea that our paths would cross at this camp. I was not even aware that he might be visiting the Dominican Republic.

It was a nice reunion for us as well as a pleasant social time for the youth from both groups. This would be the last night for the group from Michigan before returning home. They had numerous exciting mission experiences to share from the week they had just spent in ministry serving the people in this area. The weather had been perfect, the campground had been safe, and best of all there had been no mosquitoes. They left early in the morning and the camp was ours. This was truly the perfect spot for a vacation with a canopy of palm trees overhead, cool afternoon breezes blowing across waters, and picturesque colors of the fading sun across the surf in the evenings.

The big waves were fun for everyone except little four-year-old Karen. She wanted to play in the water, but the big crashing breakers were just too much for her. The following day would be her birthday and she entered a special request in honor of the day. Just a few days earlier, while en route to the campgrounds, we had passed several calm bays with beautiful beaches. Her only birthday plea was a day to play in calm waters. We packed a few things for the day in the trailer and began to retrace the highway up the coast.

We had gone only 30 or 40 minutes from camp when the Montero made its last stand. Almost without warning, the motor stopped, and we coasted to the side of the road. We were praying

Life-Saving Mosquitoes

silently for help from above and wisdom to know what to do when someone pointed to a small wooden plaque nailed to the tree right beside us. The sign proudly announced a mechanic shop in letters painted with a two inch paint brush. Fred and I caught a ride down the road to the shop—a tree with car parts all around it—to find out if the local mechanic would be of some assistance. He said he could fix the Montero, but the necessary gasket would have to be purchased in a city three hours away. The repairs would take a couple of days with travel for parts and the necessary repairs. We had no other option but to invite him to proceed, and we promised him we would return early the following week.

We were able to catch rides back to the camp, accepting the fact that we would be on foot for only the next day or two. By the time all of us got back to camp, it was late afternoon. We did the best we could to make the day special for Karen, but had a very limited supply of birthday items for small girls.

Youthful minds can often be quite creative as was the case in this situation lacking entertainment. They decided to make up a program full of skits and songs for the adults that night, and they went to work preparing for the Christian Drama Hour. The electricity had been off for the afternoon, which was nothing out of the ordinary, but not to worry as the camp had a generator. It was just getting dark when the generator that had been working perfectly throughout the afternoon sputtered and quit. After a little investigation of all the obvious things that might be causing the problem, like sufficient gas and proper spark to the plug, it became evident that something deeper was causing the problem. The generator would also need to wait for repair before it could be used again. "That's great," thought the producers of the evening's activities "Now we will have to perform in the dark." Now the search for torches for the night would be the business at hand. If it worked for Caesar's actors, it would work for them as well, they concluded.

Just as it got dark and time for the show to start, a cloud of mosquitoes came into the campgrounds with such a vengeance that we literally had to flee on the run. "Where did all these mosquitoes come from?" we wondered. We hadn't seen any mosquitoes all week. There was nothing to do but shut the doors and windows tight, turn out

I Will Save You to Make You a Blessing

the lights, and hide from the merciless attackers. We were all in one large room filled with bunk beds. It was pitch black, and the best protection from our insect attackers seemed to be under the covers of our beds. Someone called out in the dark, "Are we just going to go to sleep? It's only eight o clock." The thick clouds of mosquitoes had pretty much removed all our options. For lack of anything else to do, everyone just fell asleep.

We woke up early with more than a full night's sleep and dressed for church. We walked partway and caught a bus the rest of the way to the closest town. We found a little church and had a nice time worshiping with our Christian brothers and sisters who happened to live on a little island many miles from where we had grown up. Truly, there is a spirit of unity in God's house that cannot be found anywhere else.

After church, we caught the bus back to the long, sandy road that led us to the campgrounds and began to hike in. We had only walked about a mile when we saw a group of people walking in our direction. They were wailing and mourning, sobbing and crying, and waving their arms in obvious distress. The closer this group came to us the more evident it became that something was seriously wrong! When the sobbing and wailing group met us in the road, David asked them what was the matter. Through their sobs they began to recount the horrific night they had just encountered.

A group of bandits dressed as women and armed with guns, knives and broken bottles, had come down this very road the night before. They stopped at each house on both sides of the road to collect all the money and valuables that they could extract from their poor victims. These drunken bandits would break into a house demanding money. If they didn't have enough or get it fast enough they would grab the children and begin to slash their legs and arms with the broken bottles. When they were finished, they would destroy the home even knocking some of them completely to the ground. Women were beaten; others had been stabbed with large knives, leaving at least one man dead. These men in women's clothing stopped at nothing in their demonic state of mind. "It's a good thing they didn't know you were staying at the camp last night, or you would have been a prime target," they said as they turned to continue on their way.

Life-Saving Mosquitoes

The band of sad mourners slowly walked away, leaving us in a state of shock. We tried not to think of what might have happened to our little group of missionaries had these demon-possessed men known we were there. Some of God's Word spoke to us in ways that it never had before. We could sense the reality of verses like "You will not be afraid of the terror by night, or of the arrow that flies by day, of the pestilence that stalks in darkness, or of the destruction that lays waste at noon, a thousand may fall at your side and ten thousand at your right hand, but it shall not approach you"(Psalms 91:5-7), and "For He will give His angels charge concerning you, to guard you in all your ways. They will bear you up in their hands that you do not strike your foot against a stone"(Psalms 91:11). Without a doubt a wall of heavenly angels stood guard around our campsite that night.

As we walked along the sandy road back to the campgrounds the reality of what God had done for us began to sink in. The statement from the mourning villagers kept playing and replaying in our minds. "If those men had known you were there, who knows what they would have done to you and your family." All at once we could see the events of our lives in a very different light; everything that had seemed so mysterious and difficult just the night before had been part of a plan to save our lives. If the Montero had not broken down at the exact time and place that it had, it would have been parked out in front of our room, announcing our presence. If the generator would have kept running the night before, the lights would have made indoor activities a reality and surely would have betrayed us. The mosquitoes were perhaps the most life-saving of all due to the way they had so totally restricted our freedom. We could not help praising God for the difficulties that turned out to be blessings in disguise.

I am so glad for a God who sits enthroned far above the distractions of our world; a God who can see clearly the end from the beginning. I am sure that someday everything that may be perplexing in our lives today, all the questions and trials we have faced, will be made plain. We will then see the entire plan a loving God had for our lives. I am convinced that not one of us will look back desiring to change even one of the divine providences that seem so difficult for us today. We will then be able to see the beauty of His plan from beginning to end. Our praise and worship will only grow richer and

I Will Save You to Make You a Blessing

deeper in that land of glory as our understanding is illuminated concerning all that He has worked in our behalf while on life's journey. Let's not wait until we are face to face before we begin praising Him. We are told that God inhabits the praises of His children. Let's provide Him a generous habitation as we lift our voices in songs and praise along with the angels of glory.

12
Fiery Darts of the Devil

As we continued our walk back to the campgrounds, we praised God over and over for His protection and deliverance the night before. We were so glad that our God did not slumber or sleep but had commissioned his angels to encircle our little campsite. With thoughts of the night's activities, the smile that was always on Virginia's face quickly faded, and a worried expression of anxiousness came in its place.

An overwhelming sense of fear seemed to fill her mind. She instantly became restless and fearful for her children even though it was early afternoon, and the men from the night before were long gone and most certainly would not come back to revisit the same crime scene the following day. Virginia had become almost immobilized as she sat and stared, not wanting to participate in anything. This started to become a major distraction for David as he was making last minute preparations for evangelistic meetings that would begin soon after our return from vacation.

Nightfall came and darkness replaced the sunshine, only increasing the anxiety in Virginia's heart. She lay awake all night imagining every rustling leaf was the sound of an attacker trying to sneak into her room. Every time a dog barked, she would grab David just as he was ready to doze off to sleep from the last session of fearfulness, and say, "Did you hear that? Those dogs saw something out there." This situation would be bad enough anywhere, but it seemed that every family had at least two or three dogs that had been waiting all day to join a neighborhood forum to discuss and express the frustrations of the previous day.

You can only imagine the condition of this family as they came to eat breakfast the next morning. Without sleep, Virginia's condition definitely lacked any signs of improvement. David's eyes were puffy and red even though he attempted an occasional smile. The children had slept through some of the fearful outbursts of the night but definitely were not daisy-fresh from a peaceful night's sleep. It was obvious that the sooner we could return to the school, the better it would be for all of us.

Fred and I found a ride to the mechanic's roadside oasis to check the repair status of the Montero. He had just received the necessary parts and promised to have our transportation ready the next day. It was a long day and night, but we had no other option than to wait out our time. The next day we were on our way back to the mission as promised.

It was good to be back after the stress of the past few days. With each passing day all of us became more and more concerned for David and his family. The panic and anxiety had not remained back at the campground. The sound of rustling leaves in the trees around their home caused the same confusion each night that it had at the campsite. Virginia's condition had formed a pattern that must be interrupted. It was now a matter of days until David would be standing up to share the gospel with people from all the surrounding region, and his condition was deteriorating rapidly with each sleepless night.

As a registered nurse, Sherry watched what was taking place from a medical perspective. She called some of us to look at the symptoms outlined in one of her medical books for anxiety attacks, or sometimes known as panic attacks. Virginia had scored almost a 100% of the symptoms from the list. We knew something would have to be done soon, as Sherry's days were filled with taking Virginia's blood pressure, taking her to a local clinic for supposed heart attacks, difficulty breathing and many other life-threatening conditions that existed in her mind.

An emergency trip to Santo Domingo to see a specialist became the top priority if any degree of focus was to return to our little mission. In a matter of minutes the doctor reassured Virginia that her health was fine. To the rest of us he said that he was convinced that her symptoms

Fiery Darts of the Devil

were of a psychological nature and indicated very conclusively that she was experiencing anxiety attacks. Armed with only a prescription for some medication that might help, we began our trip back to the school. We were all praying that God would overrule on behalf of this special family. It was obvious that an all-out war had been declared in the spiritual realm seeking desperately to interrupt the sharing of the gospel. We could clearly see that as the Bible says, fiery darts were being hurled at David and his family that were intended to make it impossible for him to have the composure and concentration to be able to preach.

It was dark and getting late as we approached the little town that would be the site for the upcoming meetings in a few days. We were all anxious to get back to the school and hoping David and his family could experience their first restful night's sleep in days.

As we came around the last bend in the road, we could see flames shooting high in the air, making it impossible for anyone to continue. Cars, trucks, buses, and vehicles of all kinds were backed up for a long distance behind the flames. We parked with the other stranded motorists and walked to the fire to see what the problem was. Not only was a huge bonfire raging across the road, but large pieces of steel, logs, and anything that could be used to form a barricade had been dragged and piled in the way, evidently just in case someone might think of driving through this raging inferno with flames leaping high into the sky. Perhaps the creators of this display thought it possible that someone may happen along desiring to test the theory that a gas tank really would explode at 2,000 degrees and attempt such a test at their site. The fine collection of large obstacles blocking the road in front of the fire, however, would prohibit this sort of test from transpiring at their inferno.

The timing of all this was too significant to miss. The devil was on an all-out campaign to halt any advances of the kingdom of God. We knew there were no other side roads that could be taken from any other point, even if we made a considerable backtrack. We needed to pass directly through this town to reach the little side road that led to the school. We were stranded!

Sherry walked to the local pastor's house with Virginia and the children, while David and I talked to people around the fire to find out what was going on. This fire had been started as a strike against gov-

I Will Save You to Make You a Blessing

ernment corruption that had been acted out against some of the residents of this town. People were angry at the injustice that they had been victims to. The free-flowing rum that found its way to occasions like this did nothing to calm the situation. It was obvious that there were no plans for anything to change anytime soon as the police and military were not anxious to deal with a mob.

We began inquiring if some other road might exist that we didn't know about. There was none. We continued to ask people if there might be some route that we could take that would allow us to bypass this point and continue on our way.

One young man said, "I know a way that you can bypass all this; I'll show you the way." He walked back to the waiting Montero with David and me. He said, "I used to work for the Cuban sugarcane farmer up the road a little ways, and his cane field is the only thing separating you from another road that comes into the other side of town."

We came to the large cane plantation that we often passed on our way to Santo Domingo and turned off onto a dirt path leading to a large gate. The young man got out and opened the gate, allowing us to enter. A tractor path with deep ruts shone in the moonlight; this would be the bypass that connected us to the other road. He seemed a little less confident now than he had back at the fire as he said, "I think you can make it." We wondered what he meant, but not for long. This tractor path had been used in some very wet conditions that left ruts deeper than our wheels.

The path wound back and forth, and soon we were riding on top of ridges that began to cross from side to side making it impossible to follow. This narrow path had long since taken us past the point of being able to retreat. It was just wide enough for us to pass, making turning around impossible. In the darkness I knew there would be no way to negotiate the way we had just come in reverse. There was only one thing to do, keep going and hope things would get better. It was clear that things were not getting better, however, as the narrow ridges became impossible to negotiate.

With a loud thud and the singing of spinning tires, we sat with all four tires suspended in air and the body of the Montero resting comfortably on a high ridge in the center of the path. We got out and assessed the situation to see if there was anything we might be able to do as a possible remedy. Without a crane we were hopelessly stuck. After spending a moment looking up and down the sugarcane fields for the needed crane we concluded that the probability of one poised and ready to lift us out of our predicament was rather slim. It seemed fairly conclusive, after our brief evaluation, to say we were stuck!

I remember looking up into the clear starry night talking to the One who had created all the host of them by the word of His mouth. "Lord, You know all we have been through, and I know You see us stuck way out here in the middle of this field. Please, help us to find a way out of this mess; You know how much we need to get back tonight. Lord, the timing of all this is just too big to miss; don't allow Your enemy to gain a victory in further complicating the meetings that You have helped us work so hard to prepare for."

A very special peace came to surround us as we began our long walk out of the cane field. A sense of God's presence let us know He had not forgotten us. It was getting late as we walked into the yard of the large plantation, hoping someone might still be awake who would be able to help us. Two young men sitting in the yard said the plantation owner had gone to the city for the day and had not returned yet. We sat and waited, hoping he wouldn't decide to spend the night in the city. We kept our eye on the large four wheel drive tractor that sat parked in the driveway. This John Deere looked like it could climb a mountain, and that's about what we needed at the moment. Soon the lights of an approaching truck announced the arrival of the man who held the key to the tractor parked in the driveway. He was a friendly man, for which we were grateful, since we were parked in the middle of his field late at night without his permission.

The young man acting as our guide graciously took responsibility for the situation, for which we were also grateful. As the farmer listened to our plight, his eyes got big and he said, "You were taking them through where?" There was a slight pause in his friendly spirit as he spoke in no uncertain terms to a young man who had no business acting as a guide through someone else's property.

He said, "There is no way you could have made it through that field in a jeep." Grabbing a chain he said, "Come with me. I think you will see what I mean." He drove the John Deere to the spot where we were stuck and hooked our bumper to the tractor with

I Will Save You to Make You a Blessing

his chain.

The giant tractor soon had us skidding along the path. Sometimes the wheels were touching the ground and sometimes they were dangling in the air. It was a little bit like being on a sled towed through the snow, except for the grinding sounds of the rocks and dirt underneath us. The further we skidded down this tractor path, the more we agreed with his assessment; this was no place at all for anything other than the giant four wheel drive tractor ahead of us. Evidently, some of the pavement had vanished from this super highway since our young guide had last made his journey effortlessly across this field. We soon came to a marshy area that sent the huge tractor down to the axles in mud and slime, leaving us trailing behind like a sled in tow. This was quite an adventure in itself, sloshing through the muck, listening to the gurgling sounds of our jeep-sled, and watching our headlights bobbing up and down like a cork on rough seas.

After being dragged along through the marsh for quite a ways, we came to a river running along the edge of the field. Down into the river plunged the giant tractor with us chained behind. We felt like we were on an inner tube that was only half inflated, attempting to be towed behind a giant ski boat, half sinking and half floating. The gurgling sound of water pouring in around our feet reminded us that Montero's are better land vehicles than sea-going vessels. We prayed that the chain pulling us forward would not come loose as we felt the current arguing with it, causing us to sway from side to side like a cork on a string in a brook. As we came up on the other bank and onto dry land again, we thanked the farmer for his kindness. He said, "You are welcome, but please don't drive through here again." We assured him we had no plans for any such moonlight drives in the future.

We praised the Lord as we pulled up on the pavement and headed into town from the opposite direction. We went as quietly as possible past the remains of other smoldering fires from the day's demonstration, making a circuitous route to avoid the mob at the other end of town. Most of the town was sleeping as we carried the children to their waiting ride and continued on to the school.

The fire on the road and the activities of the night had done little to calm Virginia's fears and reassure her that she was safe and secure in this foreign country. The devil had carefully aimed his darts at a target that would do the most calculated damage to God's cause. The students were coming back, the meetings were scheduled to begin, and David had not had more than a few naps in many days; God would have to provide special strength for His servant.

Most of us are not aware of the real battles that God's servants encounter as they give their lives in service for Him. Let's begin a pattern of affirmation rather than a spirit of criticism for those who are leading the way in the cause of God. Maybe right now would be a good time to lift up one of these special people in prayer. Your pastor would be glad to be added to your list, I'm sure.

13
A Valiant Evangelist

David was now totally exhausted from the numerous sleepless nights. He tried to bravely smile and move on in faith that God would give him the strength to share the gospel with power and authority. It appeared to the rest of us that David was living on strength from heaven alone as the opening evening arrived. With our multipurpose trailer in tow, we provided first class taxi service for the neighbors waiting along the road. We pulled up in front of the university that was to be the site for our meetings with double or triple the normal passenger capacity in our Mitsubishi Montero. But who could say what would be considered normal? The large trailer was loaded with bodies much like sardines in a can. People seemed to be coming from everywhere, and within just a few minutes the lecture hall was full of people.

The people seemed eager to hear a message of hope in a country where hopelessness was all that many had ever known. No one would have ever known the state of exhaustion that the preacher was experiencing as he poured his heart and soul into his opening presentation. At the conclusion of the first meeting, all were invited to come back for an entire series on themes of salvation. Hundreds of people came night after night to listen as David preached of a crucified and risen Savior.

In a desperate attempt to weaken God's servant, the devil continued relentlessly to disrupt David's every attempt to sleep. Each day was a new struggle to continue on in a state of exhaustion. The more earnestly David preached, the more zealous were the nightly interruptions from fear and anxiety. A real battle was taking place right before

A Valiant Evangelist

our eyes. The one that began the war against the government of God in heaven was continuing the battle for souls. For the moment, David appeared to be a key target as he invited men and women to accept God's gift of salvation and experience a new life of freedom in Christ.

Large numbers of people continued to fill the lecture hall night after night. It seemed plain to see that the devil was not about to give up as the meetings progressed. If he could not silence the preacher by means of exhaustion and fatigue, he would attack from a different direction. Without any warning, the school administrator informed us that our contract for the use of the building had been canceled. Tonight would be our last night to use this facility.

"What would You have us do now, Lord?" we all prayed silently. It was not difficult to see that a new form of attack had come to attempt a halt to the spread of the gospel. David said, "I refuse to quit or give up. As long as I have breath, I am going to preach." As we prayed and wondered what to do, an elementary school teacher who had been attending the meetings overheard our dilemma and offered the use of her backyard for the remaining meetings. At the close of the meeting, we informed our audience we would be terminating the meetings at the university and moving to a new location.

The next afternoon we went to evaluate the backyard auditorium that would be the site for the conclusion of our meetings. Our hearts dropped as we stepped into the backyard of this humble little home. Only those familiar with the conditions in a rural and impoverished setting such as this could fully appreciate our new auditorium. Chickens, dogs, and cats were there to pave the way for those that might choose to join them later in the evening. A yard consisting of a few sprigs of grass seasoned with generous proportions of dirt, mud, and other interesting substances would be our carpet underfoot. The walls on either side of our backyard auditorium were thorn bushes with barbed wire woven strategically in and around and through the branches. The wire was a multipurpose variety that could be used to dry clothes, hold up strings of Christmas lights during the holiday season, and other useful purposes. But the primary function of the wire would be to keep the squealing, snorting, grunting pigs from free passage into our side of the yard and becoming casual meeting attendees. The thorn bush, wire filled walls and earthen carpeting were not the only items that added to

I Will Save You to Make You a Blessing

the decorum. A large tree gave the singing birds a comfortable balcony seat and a chance to sit right in the center of the yard, joining the meetings from the balcony section of our auditorium.

We hung some electrical cords, stretching them from the tree to the house for a light or two that would probably go off anyway with the constant interruption of electricity. A little keyboard was set up on one side of the backyard by Sherry, our music committee. We moved a small stand into position for David to use as a podium. We prayed that God would change a backyard full of animals, birds, and other distractions into an auditorium filled with heavenly angels and an abundant measure of His Spirit.

We learned that the same priest who had been working so fervently against us earlier, had the power to open or close any door he should choose. He simply informed the university that we couldn't use the building any longer, and they dared not disagree with the one that controlled not only this town but a whole sector of the country. He was definitely a man of authority in this little town, even carrying a pistol when he was out and about. The enemy certainly did not want these meetings to continue! All of us agreed, we would continue even if just one person would accept salvation from Jesus. How could we quit if He would have been willing to leave heaven just for you or me?

We did our best not to appear discouraged when so few of the people attending made the transition to the new backyard auditorium. We knew very well that many in our previous audience probably had been warned not to attend.

The singing began with those that came to hear the conclusion of the gospel messages. Sometimes the singing and preaching had background music supplied by the squealing pigs just on the other side of the fence. Often, other forms of life would come passing through the arena, but the people didn't seem to even notice, so we decided not to pay any attention either. At the conclusion of the meetings, when David invited those that would like to make a full surrender to Jesus and take their stand in baptism to come to the front, several people came forward. The lady that owned the humble little home was one of the first to take her stand. God had accomplished a victory, overruling every one of the devil's fiery darts intended to keep men and women from hearing the gospel. New names were written in the "Lamb's Book of Life."

A Valiant Evangelist

This battle will soon end and each register will stand for eternity. Have you invited anyone to join you in singing the victory song around the throne of God? Maybe today you should make friends with someone who has not yet been invited to the banquet and invite them to join you for an eternity of blessings; tell them it's free for the asking, a gift that a loving Heavenly Father desires just for them.

An Amazing Journey, What A Blessing

Our river swimming pool.
(Dominican Republic)

Our five jungle home school attendees from left to right: Seth, Dustin, Jacqlyn, Rachel and Sasha.
(Dominican Republic)

Our gardens after much hard work.
(Dominican Republic)

The rest room facilities in place and ready to use upon our arrival.
(Dominican Republic)

Some of our neighbors standing in front of their outdoor kitchen.
(Dominican Republic)

The Montero and trailer loading neighbors in route to evangelistic meetings: standing in front from left to right are David Cruz, a local pastor, and Virginia Cruz.
(Dominican Republic)

Fred Flint sitting in front of the 8' by 10' room that he lived in for seven years until his marriage to Maria.
(Dominican Republic)

One of our neighbors' houses.
(Dominican Republic)

A picture of our garden in full bloom with Fred Flint, Sasha, and Dustin.
(Dominican Republic)

Our students enrolled in conversational
English in a nearby village.
(Dominican Republic)

Rachel, Sasha, and Jacqlyn sharing food with neighbors.
(Dominican Republic)

An underground prison used by the Sandanistas in the civil war to house scores of prisoners in a single room. The small opening in the wall is the only air supply which is fed by a shaft to the surface.
(Nicaragua)

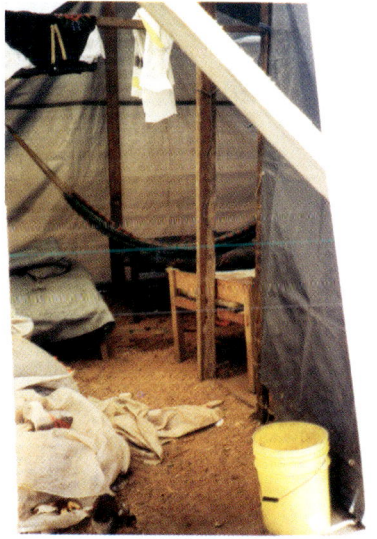

Inside a refugee shelter.
(Nicaragua)

Our pet parrot contemplating breakfast.
(Dominican Republic)

The remains of some homes on Main St. in Wiwili
3 weeks after hurricane Mitch.
(Nicaragua)

Wiwili: the smell right here was incredible.
(Nicaragua)

The only piece of equipment in the town for removing the mud—it was out of commission.
(Nicaragua)

The waiting area for our medical clinic for refugees.
(Nicaragua)

More of Wiwili.
(Nicaragua)

A missing casket after the flood—several
were washed down stream.
(Nicaragua)

Remains of another house in Wiwili.
(Nicaragua)

14

Our God is Faithful

Many other stories could be included from our time in the Dominican Republic, but I will close this portion of our lives with just a comment or two.

Virginia's health made an immediate return to Mexico a necessity. The people in the surrounding community truly hated to see this family return to Mexico. Their ministry, characterized by love and compassion, left impressions that will last a lifetime. The sudden change in plans for David and his family did not deter them in the least as servants of God. As soon as they returned to their home, they started a new ministry in a remote part of Mexico for a group of Indians that had never before heard the story of Jesus. Virginia's health returned soon after going home, allowing her to take a strong leadership role for the Lord once again.

A few months after David and his family left, we knew it was time for us to return to the United States in order to provide the jungle home school attendees a more formal education. At the conclusion of our second school year at the little mission, it became clear that we needed to make plans to return to Wisconsin.

It was an incredible challenge and sacrifice for Fred when he made the decision to stay as the new director of this little school. It seemed that it would be nearly impossible for a young eligible bachelor to meet the companion of his dreams in such a far removed spot on planet Earth. God did not answer Fred's prayers immediately, but in His time He did answer in a wonderful way. After Fred had waited patiently for several years, God sent a young lady named Maria to serve

I Will Save You to Make You a Blessing

as a missionary at the same mission that Fred was directing, literally landing the answer to his prayers on his doorstep. Once again it might be observed that the things in life that have the greatest value often require a great deal of patience. The day Fred and Maria walked down the aisle to be married, you would have had a difficult time convincing either of them that waiting and following God's leading was not a wonderful way to go.

Sherry really enjoyed life as a missionary. When we decided to return home, she decided to stay a little longer, encouraging God's work on this beautiful island. Perhaps the palm trees, tropical fruits, and warm sunny skies influenced her decision as she thought about the deep winter snows and sub-zero temperatures that would greet her if she should return to Wisconsin. After spending one more year helping in various ways in the Dominican Republic, Sherry decided to extend her missionary experience by moving to Africa, assisting our parents as they worked for the people they loved so much. Working for others is truly a rewarding experience; if the opportunity becomes available to you, make sure and take it.

I would be missing a wonderful opportunity if I didn't share this last thought from the Dominican Republic. When it came time to leave, the Lord spoke to me in a very personal way. Often the Lord uses passages from His Word when He wants to communicate with us, as was the case this time. "He said unto them, when I sent you without purse, and scrip, and shoes, lacked ye any thing? And they said, nothing" (Luke 22:35). I wish it were possible for me to convey the loving and personal way that the Lord spoke these words to me. At that moment, I felt a wave of His love come washing over me. We went to the Dominican Republic without the monthly support of any organization or church; we went simply because the Lord strongly impressed us that it was His first choice for us, and He would bless us. He now desired that I should re-examine some of these blessings, as He invited me to stop and look back for a moment with Him. As numerous providences replayed in my mind in rapid succession, I was overwhelmed with a sense of gratitude. God often desires that we stop and reflect on the many blessings He sends to us each day. It is always an encouragement to look back and review God's past blessings and mercies.

God provided for us in ways that could never be interpreted as

Our God is Faithful

coincidental. God impressed people we had never met to send money for the support of our little mission project when they learned of this venture of faith. Friends and family sent gifts from time to time that always arrived in such a timely manner that we knew God was definitely the One in charge of our lives.

In a very providential meeting in Santo Domingo, I met a supervisor from the Dole Pineapple Plantation located just a few miles out of the city. He was in desperate need of some stainless steel pipe welding for an expansion project in their juice factory. He simply hadn't been able to locate any welders with the knowledge or skill for the task. I had only visited this store on one other occasion prior to this visit. Some might say I just happened to come on the right day at the right moment, but I could see the coincidence was too timely to have happened by chance. The plant supervisor was just preparing to walk out the door when I walked in. The salesman he had been talking with looked over at me and asked if I knew anyone who might be able to help him with such a specialized project. I informed him that he just happened to be talking to someone with ten years of experience in the very type of work that he needed to have done. Dole was willing to pay both a premium wage and supply all the fresh pineapple I could stack in the Montero for each visit to the plant. As always, these funds came at just the right time to keep our expenses paid in a timely manner. A mountain of fresh pineapple after each visit also did wonders for our fresh fruit department at the school.

Do you think I could be persuaded that all of these strange coincidences happened because the stars were aligned just right? It would be impossible for me to be convinced that it was not the maker of the stars providing for our needs by the providences of His hand! God's timing is always perfect! No one at the little mission ever had to go without a meal during the time we spent with them. The students came from poor families making it impossible for them to pay for any of their personal expenses or even something as basic as food. I want to assure you that when they came to the table they meant business. Our Father proved over and over that He knows how to take care of His own. God was telling me, "It is time for you to go home now, but I want you to stop and look at the way I have taken care of you and all these students." I felt the warmth of my Heavenly Father's presence as he took me on a mental tour of His many providences. At this moment I felt like a royal son of the King of the Universe.

The summer before we returned to the United State,s my father came for a visit while on furlough from his mission responsibilities in Africa. We appreciated the numerous improvements he made during his brief visit to our little school. After a few weeks he said, "I think it's time for me to go back to Africa where life is easier." He really wasn't kidding either. We experienced some very interesting challenges just in the few weeks he was visiting that no doubt helped shape his assessment. One night the Montero quit several miles from the school, resulting in a long hike through deep mud and rugged terrain in the darkness. This experience, among others, could possibly have contributed to his assessment.

Before he left he handed me a sealed envelope with several hundred dollars in it. He said, "This is only to be opened as a last resort if all other means have been exhausted and you are in an emergency situation." I thought about that envelope from time to time throughout the next year, but always before I could justifiably open the envelope, God would provide enough to more than pay for our immediate needs. As God spoke the words of the scripture mentioned above, I couldn't help thinking of the envelope that was still unopened in my room. We never opened this special envelope until after we arrived back in our homeland. What an inspiration my family has been to me; walking the pathway of faith before me as courageous soldiers of the cross.

I would like to add an affirmation of God's faithfulness with a generational testimony. My grandfather was a cowboy on the plains of North Dakota in his younger years. His parents died when he was quite young, leaving him to face life all alone. He was living a work-hard-drink-hard life until divine providence interrupted his meaningless search for happiness.

One night as he was riding home on his horse he spotted many carriages and horses outside the old country school house. The brightly lit, well attended schoolhouse would surely be holding a dance and he was not about to pass up an opportunity like that. He tied up his horse and walked over to the window. He peered in, expecting to see and hear a dance with a round of music beginning at any moment. As he approached the window, he heard someone speaking, instead. Some-

Our God is Faithful

thing the traveling evangelist said that night kept him listening for the rest of the night's presentation, but he never went inside. Several nights he returned as the unobserved window attendee desiring to learn more but not having the courage to go inside. He felt the drawing power of the gospel as he returned night after night.

At the conclusion of the meetings, he made his decision to follow Jesus all the way in baptism. His life and his home were never the same from the moment Jesus came into his heart. My grandparents became dedicated Christians, raising ten children who would all follow their parents as soldiers of the cross. I am sharing this abbreviated account with you in order to pass on a testimony of God's faithfulness. I am not sure if my grandfather was thinking of a family blessing as in the days of the patriarchs and prophets when he shared a scripture blessing with my father to pass down to succeeding generations. My father has confirmed the validity of this scripture promise to me, and I would now like to pass it on to you. Psalms 37:25 reads as follows, "I have been young and now am old, yet I have never seen the righteous forsaken or his descendants begging bread."

If you have allowed your Heavenly Father to adopt you into His royal family, you too, will be able to agree with the psalmist and my grandfather. My Heavenly Father flooded my mind with many of these special thoughts as He replayed the many evidences of His faithfulness to a family that had stepped out in faith to follow His leading.

I'm so thankful to be able to bring back a good report from a distant land as well as a generational testimony of God's faithfulness. Truly, our heavenly Father is a faithful Father! This may be a good time to spend a moment or two just recounting the many evidences of God's faithfulness in your life. I am sure you will discover a wonderful new courage for your present struggles as well as the challenges ahead. Remember, every one of God's biddings will be an enabling to move forward as He empowers us with His blessings and strength. If God invites you to work for Him, don't miss the adventure, He has promised us, "I will never leave you or forsake you" (Hebrews 13:5).

15

Praising God in the Storm

Ministry is a much more difficult task in countries that abound in blessing, like the United States, than in countries that have so very little. Being increased with goods and feeling a need of nothing is a spiritual poverty that creates one of the most difficult mission fields remaining in the world today. When we returned home, we prayed that God would show us where He wanted us to work in this most challenging mission field of affluence.

Wisconsin Academy (a Christian boarding school) provided our own high school age students a place to continue their education as well as many opportunities for us to work with and for other young people searching to discover a relationship with God for themselves. Working with youth can be one of the most challenging and rewarding ministries. We have always been thankful that God assigned us to such an enjoyable mission station.

An added responsibility that God has blessed us with is encouraging His people to pray. This assignment has proven to be the most difficult of the two in a country that has been blessed so abundantly. Many Christians have little or no prayer experience at all; after all, why pray? I have everything I want and more. Although most of us would not openly admit to this mindset, we act it out every day. We rush from task to task in such a frantic pace throughout the day and then collapse at night with scarcely a thought of a kind and loving Father who has waited all day for an intimate moment with us.

As you have perhaps been able to see, prayer has been an experience that has blessed and shaped my life in so many ways I can

Praising God in the Storm

scarcely begin to count them all. When you begin to realize that prayer has everything to do with enjoying the presence of God throughout each day, and little to do with asking for more things, you need little prompting to come immediately back to the One who surrounded you with an atmosphere of peace and light the day before. Much of our time is filled with visiting churches, schools, prisons, and homes, encouraging others to enjoy this aspect of their walk with God.

"Praising God in the Storm" is an experience that happened to me just after returning from a prayer conference at Canadian University College. Mark Crary and I were just completing a kitchen remodeling project in Sun Prairie, Wisconsin, one November when God chose to reinforce a powerful principle in my life. It was late in the afternoon with just enough time to haul all the old, dead kitchen components that had been replaced with new ones to a local landfill. (For those who may lack current information on the subject of landfills, a landfill is the politically correct term for what has been termed a "dump" in less sophisticated times.) Mark and I loaded a tandem trailer behind my pickup with all the unwanted items that were being replaced in the remodeling project. My watch indicated there would be just enough time to make it to the landfill before the four o'clock closing time. Anticipating an additional stop at the hardware store after emptying the trailer, I removed my outer layer of work clothes in order to have a cleaner appearance at the store.

It was only a short drive to the landfill, which had grown over time to be one of those garbage mountains that have become familiar objects near many cities. I pulled up on the large truck scales to be weighed in with my load in order to determine the charges that would be based on the number of pounds that I would deposit on Garbage Mountain. I followed the road that wound its way around the giant mound of decaying matter to deposit my trailer full of goods and make the mountain just a little bit taller.

Pulling into the dumping area at the top of the mountain, I met a giant bulldozer with huge steel cleats on wheels as tall as the cab of my pickup sitting in position, ready to push loads of garbage to just the right location after each contributor pulled away from the deposit zone to descend the mountain. Some of you, perhaps, are of the misguided opinion that garbage mountains are constructed with the random distri-

I Will Save You to Make You a Blessing

bution of refuse, but I want to assure you that the dump engineer operating the giant dozer puts each contribution in the exact location that he knows will create a perfect mountain. Perhaps this added insight will contribute to a new appreciation of the next garbage mountain you pass by. Countless travelers pass these architectural compositions with scarcely a thought as to the planning and calculating that has transpired in order to turn garbage into a masterpiece.

There were several large trucks lined up awaiting the opportunity to make a contribution in the main unloading area. The dozer operator motioned for me to back in on the far right side of the numerous garbage trucks in the process of unloading. Responding in complete faith in the competency of the chief engineer at hand, I turned around and backed into the area he indicated. As I got out of the truck to unload the trailer, I was horrified as I looked all around and under my truck and trailer. The person just preceding me in this spot had dumped a large load of old shingles loaded with nails, covering the ground under my truck and trailer. I knew I didn't have a spare tire for the trailer, and the truck spare stored up under the truck bed for several years had never been removed from its resting place. I was almost certain that the winter salt used for de-icing the Wisconsin highways would have the truck spare nicely rusted in place.

I flew to the trailer to try to make the unloading resemble a pit stop at the Indy 500. I frantically threw the contents in all directions—no doubt to the dismay of the one planning the organization of my discarded goods—from the trailer and ran back to the truck to quickly escape the mountain before the air could escape my tires. But my fast unloading techniques were not fast enough. My fears became a reality with the rear tire on the driver's side completely flat and sitting on the rim pushed deep into the decaying matter.

Instantly, some very unflattering thoughts entered my mind concerning the one that had directed me to this bed of nails. The sun was getting low, and the evening air was already quite cool in late November. I looked at the clean clothes that I had on, remembering the overalls I had removed just before coming here. My eyes then looked down at the layers of filth and decaying matter that I would soon be lying on in order to change the flat tire before me. The more I thought about my situation, the angrier I became. I lifted the hood to remove the jack from its storage place. The jack had also never been removed from its original clamp. The threads were literally frozen with rust from the winter salt baths it had encountered.

After several attempts to free the frozen threads, I finally got the wing nut to move with great effort. The remaining problem was that there were two inches of fine threads to unscrew in order to free the jack from the clamp that held it fast. With each revolution of the wing nut the list of uncomplimentary thoughts accumulated. Finally, the jack was free and positioned under the axle to lift the sunken wheel from its grave in the muck. I put the jack in position and began jacking, expecting to see the truck begin to slowly rise with each pump of the jack. Isn't that what's supposed to happen? To my dismay, the truck remained buried in the layers of decaying matter, and my jack was just lowering itself slowly downward. It was getting dark and cold; my situation was becoming less and less humorous by the minute. After a little dump search, I was able to find some old boards to position under the jack and begin the jacking process once again.

With the truck jacked as high as it would go, there was just enough space for my body to slide under the truck to try to free the spare tire. This was seeming like less and less fun all the time. There was no place to escape the smell with my head wedged between the truck frame and loathsome debris underneath me. I wondered what kinds of once-living things could possibly create such a toxic odor as I felt the earth sponging up and down beneath me. There was no escaping this position if I was going to free the spare tire.

I put the tire iron in the socket and began to pry on the large nut holding the tire in place. Why did I think these threads should be any different than the others under the hood? These were just that much closer to the road and a highway salt bath from many a winter. I pulled frantically on the tire iron, only achieving a few small rotations of the nut. I wondered how long this process would take with several inches of threads to conquer before the tire could drop from its lodging place. The unpleasant and uncomplimentary thoughts for the one responsible for all this had not begun to diminish.

It was at this moment that God spoke to me. He said, "Weren't you just at a prayer conference with Ruthie Jacobsen at the Canadian University College where those in attendance were encouraged to sing

I Will Save You to Make You a Blessing

like Paul and Silas when trouble comes? You have been telling others to sing when the storms of life burst upon them. Well, this is your trouble, this is your storm, and I want you to sing right now."

I responded, "I don't want to sing right now! I don't feel like singing right now! Lord, can't you see the mess I am in? How can I possibly sing right now? And by the way, what about that guy sitting up there in his giant dozer? He doesn't exactly make me feel like singing."

At a time when I was experiencing one of my most unholy and undeserving attitudes, I felt the Lord join me under that truck with an amazing measure of His presence. Almost instantly, I felt a calm come over me that was not my own. This is incredible Lord; You can make a sanctuary out of a place like this? I began to sing a song of praise with my head still wedged into the spongy substance beneath me. My vocal projection didn't instantly resemble that of a large church choir under there. But the longer I sang, the more powerfully I felt the presence of God and the more my singing sounded like singing, rather than someone making a faint cry for help from under a pillow. The threads started moving much more freely as I sang, and I soon had the tire free from the bracket holding it in place and out from under the truck. In my improved state of mind God continued the conversation,

"How many flat tires do you have?"

"One," I said.

"And how many spare tires do you have?" He asked.

"One," I replied. I realized instantly with eight tires and only one spare that it was truly a miracle to have only one flat tire. I continued to sing with the presence of God all around me as I replaced the flat tire with the spare tire. The Lord had so changed my attitude that I was able to drive away from this incredible episode without so much as a glance in the direction of the one responsible for my distress. I sang all the way down the mountain as I drove back to the truck scales to determine the unloaded weight of my truck and trailer.

As I pulled onto the scales, it seemed that from out of nowhere came a flood of angry feelings. The devil had just hit the replay button in my mind, creating the opportunity for me to re-experience the whole unpleasant ordeal all over again. I stormed up to the window as if the poor lady behind the counter was responsible for my fate in every particular. I proceeded to vent my frustration on her as I recounted my

Praising God in the Storm

recent experience in a rapid-fire oratory. I proceeded to pay her in a rather pronounced and emphatic manner. I walked back to the truck like an unhappy child who wants the whole world to know how unfair life has been to him.

As I closed the door and prepared to leave the scales, the Lord spoke to me again. He said, "Didn't you and I just have a victory up on that mountain? Are you going to leave this place in defeat? This lady had nothing to do with what happened up there, and you know it. You need to go back in there and apologize to her." Very sheepishly I walked back up to the window. (That means all the stomp had gone from my feet.)

For some reason, when the lady saw me returning, she did not hasten back to the window, but she did return politely to her post of duty after a moment or two. "Excuse me," I said, "I want to tell you I am sorry for the way I was just talking to you. I know that none of what just happened to me had anything to do with you. Please forgive me."

She smiled, relieved that I had not come back to fill in some missing detail of the preceding speech. "That's okay," she said with a smile. Now I was able to turn and walk back to the truck with the feeling of peace and victory once again. I couldn't keep from singing and praising the Lord all the way back to the job.

The next two days were so busy I simply could not spare the time to have my tire repaired. A couple hours of unexpected free time became available three days after my visit to the landfill, so I headed to a tire shop. I glanced at the rest of the fairly worn tires on my truck and realized I would need to replace them all before winter, so I might as well just take care of it now. I pulled into the tire store and waited for the tires to be installed. As the man completed his task and was trying to replace the spare tire up under the truck, I noticed from the waiting area that he was having some difficulty.

"Do you need a hand?" I asked.

"As a matter of fact, I do," he replied. We lifted the tire and refastened it in its rightful place.

As he was letting the truck down from the hoist, I began to tell him the story of my flat tire. He looked at me and said, "I wondered why all your tires were full of nails." It dawned on me that I had been driving on three other tires with multiple nails embedded in them.

I Will Save You to Make You a Blessing

Once again I sensed the presence of God as He said, "I held up your tires with your songs of praise." I felt so humbled by the love of a God who continues to pour out His love on such undeserving children. I just opened my heart as I drove, trying the best I could to let Him know how glad I was that He was my Father in heaven. How thankful we can be for the Holy Spirit as he translates our feeble attempts of praise and thanksgiving into the language of heaven.

I would like to leave you with a real challenge—one I hope you will try very soon. The next time a storm cloud comes your way, sing a song of praise to God. Nothing will so effectively defeat the devil's plans to discourage and immobilize you in your effectiveness for God as your song of praise in the midst of the storm. Try it. It really works!

16
Hurricane Mitch

You may remember in October, 1998, every newscast paused at the satellite image of the giant swirling mass depicting Hurricane Mitch. We watched this giant mass of swirling air, with sustained winds of 180 mph, as it became the fourth strongest hurricane ever to be recorded. Perhaps you were like so many of us watching for two long days as this swirling mass suspended its trek across the Caribbean, halting just off the coast of Central America.

Do you remember having a helpless feeling as this storm of destruction began to creep inland, pouring up to 25 inches of water per day on the helpless victims in its path? In just a matter of hours the drenched soil clinging to the sides of mountains and hills became so saturated, they simply let go their grasp and came cascading down on the villages and towns below. Do you remember the look of horror on the faces of family members that watched other family members disappear right before their eyes? What would it have been like to live in a little hut—your only protection from the storm—right beside a little stream that became a raging torrent in a matter of minutes? Do you remember the pictures of these people fleeing to higher land as their property went flowing down into the valleys?

Little streams became raging rivers that flowed together with thousands of other such streams, becoming torrents that created walls of water sometimes a hundred feet deep, erasing everything in its path. We watched for five long days and nights as this storm opened its flood gates on the helpless victims below. Nightmares became realities as loved ones and family members watched this raging torrent steal away

I Will Save You to Make You a Blessing

those that were dearest to their heart. In just five days over 10,000 people disappeared, never to come home again.

I remember the pleading eyes of little orphans, the cries for help, and haunting images of total destruction that were broadcast to all of us watching around the world, hoping that someone would care enough to come and help. As I sat in church thinking about all the pain and sorrow, I knew I would have to be one of those to respond when the call for volunteers appeared in our church bulletin from ADRA, a disaster relief agency. Renee Stellpflug, a nurse and long time family friend from our local church, and I booked immediate passage to the ADRA headquarters in Managua, Nicaragua. The dedication we witnessed in the ADRA leadership and team was truly heroic. Several ADRA team members had not had more than a few short naps in weeks. The leadership provided by ADRA in this hour of crisis was so well defined and executed that the aid from seven countries and several church aid programs from the US and around the world were all directed to ADRA for distribution.

As we made our way into the ADRA headquarters in Managua, the calls for medical care continued to come flowing in. The government constantly updated and prioritized the areas that most urgently needed help. We kept wondering what these poor people were going through; they had been isolated by flood waters without any contact from the outside world since the storm. As people would arrive, teams would be formed. Soon our assignment came. Our little team would be traveling to a remote mountain village. We loaded medicine, food, water and our personal belongings into four-wheel-drive vehicles, and we were off. I kept wondering what it would be like to arrive in a place where there would be no shelter of any kind with destruction on every side. I couldn't help wondering what we would find when we finally arrived at our little village. There would not even be a decent campground to pitch a tent, just mud as far as you could see. In our four-wheel-drive Land Cruisers, we traveled for several hours through the mountains, through swollen rivers, and sometimes around pieces of bridges that still clung to the banks. We followed what was left of roads until the road ended. Our caravan came to an immediate halt. We looked at the place where the road used to be. It was obvious that an incredible force had been at work here, totally redesigning the landscape. The flood waters simply made a series of small canyons in the place that used to be a road.

With the help of local villagers, we began our trek with all the supplies that could be carried, in order to set up our little clinic in an isolated and ravaged village that now lay covered by a sea of mud. I watched the long line of porters carrying the contents of our Land Cruisers; they looked like the pictures that you see of groups leaving base camp to climb the Himalayas. It was hot and tiring climbing up and down with a full pack through these newly made canyons.

It was almost dark when we came to the little village of Bijia Norte. What a sight. Groups of people were scattered throughout the trees, living in homemade shelters made of the blue tarps delivered by government helicopters. Somehow, many of these people could still manage a smile. The sun quickly disappeared, leaving us to create some sort of camp for the two nurses, two Peace Corp volunteers, and myself in the darkness. We had pieces of one tent that we patched together for the ladies. In the one lone building that had been spared, up on some higher ground, I found lodging. This room also stored a few bags of corn and any clothes that could be salvaged. This crude shelter allowed free passage for many uninvited guests.

The hours—or should I say minutes—that slowly crept by that night, I have permanently recorded in my mind. Two planks covered with a dirty rag crudely suspended on either end were my bed. Just two or three feet above me dangled the surviving rag-clothing of the villagers in the only remaining place of storage. As I lay down on the rag covered plank, I kept hearing the government doctor telling us that lice would be in epidemic proportions in this area. I instantly felt like everything under and around me was crawling. The floor was a mixture of dirt, pieces of the corn that had been dropped, and the evidence left behind from the nightly visitors that no doubt had a regular travel route through this rodent smorgasbord. Everything seemed to be alive and moving in this hotel. After what seemed like an eternity, I wondered how much longer it would be until the sun returned to end this nightmare.

Then it was time for the bats to come and look for the mosquitoes that had been feasting on the newcomers. In the darkness I couldn't tell how close these dive bombers were to me, but it felt like many were not

I Will Save You to Make You a Blessing

missing me by much; not to worry though, I was guarded by the hanging clothing over head. That's what I thought; laying on my back staring up into the blackness listening to the commotion below and the activity above, my peace and serenity was rudely interrupted by a large moist deposit that landed on my face. The sun did come up the next morning, but it was a long time coming.

The cows, pigs, chickens, dogs and cats were the earliest attendees to arrive before sunrise at our little mountain clinic set up under a tree in front of the lone, standing building. It was early in the morning when the people started to come. Some walked and others were carried. It was one sad case after another. The lice problem was worse than anything we could have ever dreamed possible. One little girl in particular was having severe headaches. As the nurses lifted her hair, it looked like someone had spilled flour all over her head which was literally white with lice. Another poor man was carried in deathly ill with malaria; a few short months later I would know just how he felt. A short time after my return home, I developed a serious case of malaria that took months to cure. I developed a new kind of sympathy for those suffering in remote areas without proper medical care.

The experience of one brave little boy of ten or twelve aptly depicts the sorrow and heartache that had become a reality for the people who survived this horrible ordeal. I saw him standing for long hours in the hot sun, waiting, hoping that someone might help him. When he finally reached the front of the line, he came walking slowly forward, to where a nurse and I were seated, with a blank, hollow stare on his face.

"How can we help you?" I asked.

"I have a headache," was all he said.

"Why are you here all alone? Where are your mother and father?" I continued.

He said, "My father was washed away in the storm, and my mother is very sick at home with my younger brothers and sisters." He knew he was the only hope that his little family had for survival. He was feeling the weight of a cruel world resting on his shoulders.

Instantly, I knew this young boy and his family were part of the reason the Lord had impressed Lesa to press some cash into my hand just before leaving home with the instructions to listen for God to tell me who to help with these funds. I took him aside where it was a little more private and placed some of this gift from God in his hand. In this remote part of the world where the people earn less than $200 per year, I am sure this was more money than he had ever seen before. We went to our personal food supply and made him a food basket to take home with him. The blank, hollow stare was gone. In its place, a face beaming with delight, his headache was gone as he knew he could now care for the family that was awaiting his return. How it warmed my heart to know that a kind and loving Heavenly Father heard the cry of this little boy's heart in advance, inviting my wife to be the answer to his prayer.

All day the people waited patiently for the help they so desperately needed. The sun had hidden its last rays for some time before many began their long walk home. The second night exhaustion allowed for periods of sleep even though the accommodations remained the same. As I lay on those hard planks replaying the scenes of the day, I knew that in spite of my temporary inconvenience, it felt so selfish to think of how I was feeling when this was the reality of life for those that were all around me just trying to survive. There would be no plane to take them away in a few days to another country that abounded in so many good things. How could I complain when mothers and wives, who had suddenly lost their husbands in the flood waters, were now left to try to care for large families all alone? Mothers and children camped on hillsides under large blue tarps that would be the only home they had for a long time to come. The flood had destroyed not only their homes, but their crops had simply been erased from the face of the earth. What would they say to their children when they cried for breakfast in the morning? My rag covered plank somehow didn't seem as hard as it had the night before.

The next morning I received an urgent request. I'm not really sure why the ladies were so anxious for me to work on the only outhouse that sat perched up on the side of a hill just a few feet from the little town square next to the main path to the river. It was working fine as far as I could tell. Maybe it was the curious design that attracted so much attention. It really was kind of a fascinating structure. It sat there rather proudly with only one wall, and it was the back one facing the jungle. From this elevated vantage point one could easily see all that was going on just a few feet away in the little clearing used as a temporary city center. This was an ingenious plan; one would never miss a thing while powdering her nose. And now the ladies were insistent that I ruin the view with walls and a door. I conceded, even though it would mean losing touch with the action taking place all around.

We also organized some of the men waiting around this little clinic, forming a building bee. Lumber was gathered and retrieved from homes and buildings that had been destroyed to begin building another badly needed shelter. Old bent nails were gathered while grandpas tried to pound them straight again between rocks. With many hands and a few crude tools we soon had a new framework in place.

Early one morning, as I went out to pray and study in the quiet of the jungle, I saw two young mothers with several small children camped under one of the large blue tarp shelters. It appeared they had done the best they could, without the help of any men, to shelter their families. It was so heartbreaking to hear the cries of their little children and see their total helplessness. They had nothing to protect them from the insects that abound in this environment. They had crudely tried to make beds for their little ones, but rather unsuccessfully. It was at this moment I heard the Lord's still small voice say, "Some of Lesa's love gift is for these special children of mine." It was such a joy to be the delivery person as the Lord quietly directed me to some of those in the most extreme and dire need with words of compassion for those so precious in His eyes. Oh how I wished the Master from Galilee would have come walking through this sad little village to wipe away every tear from the eyes of these hurting people.

17
Our God is a Very Present Help in Time of Need

Government officials, as well as the villagers, repeatedly talked of a town down the river a ways named Wiwili (pronounced wee-wee-lee), that was one of the most devastated in all Nicaragua. Nearly 60,000 people called this town home, but now most of it was either missing or destroyed. I knew that friends and family at home would want to see the power and destruction that this incredible storm had caused. Somehow I knew I must find a way to get to this town to videotape some of the destruction we had been hearing so much about.

The clinic was well staffed, and it seemed like the opportunity was right when I learned of a government jeep that would be coming to provide transportation for a worker the next morning. Early in the morning I joined the returning Department of Health worker as she made her way back over the washed and torn pathway to the waiting jeep. For the next three hours we wound our way through the mountains and finally to the town of Wiwili.

The bridge was completely gone, leaving only one option—to cross the fast moving river. We followed the tracks of other four wheel drive vehicles that had forged the swift and swollen river. As we came up the riverbank on the other side, a very sad sight greeted our eyes. The whole lower half of the town was just twisted steel and broken concrete jutting out of the side of the hill with broken trees embedded all around. The buildings just above the crest of the floodwaters were filled with eight to ten feet of mud. Even the school and hospital were

I Will Save You to Make You a Blessing

full of mud. Many of the people were still in a state of shock while others were beginning to try to shovel out the remains of what had been a home or little store.

I tried to capture as many of the destructive scenes as possible, but how do you capture on film a cemetery that had been ripped apart by a river ten times its normal size, even floating away some of the most recently buried caskets? How do you capture the smell of stagnant pools of water and decaying matter in the tropical sun? I did the best I could as a reporter, but the afternoon sun reminded me it was time to try to find a way back up the river to the waiting group that I left early that morning. As I looked over the descending hillside leading to the river, I spotted some long dugout canoes with little outboard motors ferrying people across a section of river that used to have a bridge. That was it. My return transportation back up the river; just the answer I had been looking for. I asked several of the men if they would be willing to take me up the river to Bijia Norte but each declined. Finally, one young man agreed to the task.

The afternoon sky was blue, and with the jungle creating sort of a lush carpet of green in every direction, this was a perfect way to make a return voyage. I settled back to enjoy an expedition that would no doubt rival an exotic jungle cruise offered by some international travel agency. As we traveled up the Coco River, we followed a path carved through deep canyons between the mountains that jutted abruptly upward on either side of its banks. The evidence of the recently raging torrents and the power and force that they can cause were all around. Huge slices of mountains were simply washed away, redefining a permanent path of the Coco River. Riding in a dugout canoe was a continual balancing act, especially as we came to narrow, swift parts of the river with rapids to contend with. We traveled for about an hour and a half without seeing many signs of civilization, just jungle and more jungle. Noticing the late afternoon sun, I asked my jungle chauffeur how much farther it was to Bijia Norte. It was not really all that comforting to hear him say he had never been this far up the river, and he didn't know for sure.

He spotted a hut on a riverbank and stopped to ask a young man if he would mind joining us to act as our guide the rest of the way up the river. The young man climbed in, taking his position at the front of the

Our God is a Very Present Help in Time of Need

canoe as our new navigator. I had to know how much farther it was to our desired destination. He said, "Bijia Norte, that's a long way up the river from here!" It was not hard to notice the worried look on the young sailor's face as he stated that he had not brought enough fuel to go much farther.

He said, "I am sorry, but I will have to turn back. I am almost out of fuel." He asked, "Would you like to get out and walk from here or return back to Wiwili with me?"

The whole idea seemed preposterous; we were in thick jungle without even a path to walk on. Both sides of the river were piled high with logs, brush, and huge boulders that had tumbled down in the ragging current a few days earlier. Get out and walk; walk where? I became more than a little concerned as the prospect of finding my way back through several miles of this tangled mess in a tropical jungle that I had never even seen before was being offered as one of my options! I pleaded with him, "At least take me a little closer than this."

As I looked at the sun low on the horizon, my concerns were only increased when I saw the dark shadows from the high mountains reminding me how quickly the sunlight would disappear. I wished now for more appropriate attire; I looked down at my slip-on dress shoes as the reality that I might be in for a long walk began to settle in. I drank my last swallow of water and wished I had brought an extra bottle for just such an emergency.

When our canoe came around one more bend in the river, the young man informed me this was all the farther he could go as he was running on fumes. He pulled over to a large sand bar and said, "Are you going to get out and walk or drift back down the river with us?"

I asked the young guide, who had joined us midway up the river, how long it would take to walk from this sand bar to Bijia Norte. He thought for a minute and said, "Probably two hours." I looked at my watch and then at the low sun on the horizon—I had less than two hours of sunlight remaining. If I went back with the canoe I would be stranded in a destroyed, mud-filled village without any hope of a ride to anywhere. I would have to try and make it on foot.

Just then two young men came walking along the river bank on a large newly-created sand bar. They agreed to show me the way to a footpath that would take me back to my waiting friends. I climbed out

I Will Save You to Make You a Blessing

of the canoe and followed these two young men who were half running and half walking. After about half an hour, they stopped and pointed to a little stream that was flowing into the river several hundred yards ahead. The stream flowed around a little island and then joined the river. They said, "Make your way over to that little island, then walk that log across to the other side, climb the bank, and you will find a narrow path that will take you back to Bijia Norte." Just like that they disappeared, and I was left alone at the river's edge.

If you have been reading this story sitting in some comfortable chair in your living room, it's time to get out of that chair and join me on a huge sand bar with high mountains on either side of you, in a place you have never been before with a disappearing sun overhead, and take this walk with me. Are you here with me? Can you see the thick jungle all around? Are you wondering how we are ever going to make it back before dark? Well, I was. I knew I would have to jog as much as possible for the next hour and a half. I found a patch of stepping stones that led me to the little island and the log spanning the water from the island to the steep bank on the other side of the river. Climbing up the steep embankment, I felt all alone and lost. There was no path, only a small cluster of banana plants and a few footprints in the mud. Now what should I do? "Follow the footprints in the mud," I thought, "maybe they will lead me to a path." Later I would learn from a villager who lived nearby that a large snake had come down out of the mountains in the storm and eaten one of their cows near this very spot. I also learned of a snake just a little ways from this spot that wrapped itself from bottom to top of a very tall tree throughout the fury of the storm.

After a few minutes of following the prints in the mud through banana plants and a jungle filled with singing insects, a path appeared. It was now time to pretend to be in top shape as I half walked and half ran for the next thirty or forty minutes in the heat of a tropical climate. My water had been gone since leaving the canoe, so there wasn't any time to be thinking about being thirsty. "Every minute counts," I kept reminding myself, "just forget about the message that your body seems desperately trying to convey." I picked up the pace from half walking and half jogging to mostly jogging, as I looked at the thick jungle that spread out before me and the shadows that began to lengthen all around me.

Our God is a Very Present Help in Time of Need

After about twenty minutes I met a man riding a small horse. Out of breath and covered in sweat, I panted, "How much farther is it to Bijia Norte?"

"Oh, about an hour and a half," he said.

"An hour and a half," I thought to myself, "I thought that's how far it was when I got to the path." This was starting to feel like a treadmill walking and running frantically but going nowhere. I kept up the pace the best I could, racing against the sun.

After another half hour had passed, I came to a refugee camp right in the path. Several blue tarps were wrapped around poles and sticks creating a very sad little community right in the path. I had to step around their homemade tents to reach the path on the other side of their camp. I felt like time was fleeing from my clock at an accelerated rate. As I passed by one of the men standing in front of his tent, I asked, "How much farther is it to Bijia Norte?"

He said, "Oh, probably an hour and a half."

I was shocked; was an hour and a half the only increment of time these people knew, or was it truly yet another hour and a half to go? The sun was now setting, and my situation was becoming more and more serious. "If I only had a flashlight, it wouldn't be so bad," I thought, but I didn't even have a match. I wondered what creatures might call this part of the world home after dark. The shadows of twilight were very quickly fading into darkness. How would I make my way across all of the washed-out portions of pathway? How would I be able to skirt the deep mudslides I had been walking around and through after total darkness blanketed the jungle?

As the last glimmers of light were fleeing from the sky, the reality of true darkness began to settle in. The clouds were thick, obscuring any possible moonlight or starlight; it was beginning to feel very dark and lonely. This was the kind of darkness that you can feel. The faintest sounds in the jungle seem magnified in the darkness. Was that an animal that might be following or just a falling leaf? I could see some vague outlines of the plants and trees on either side of me, creating many possibilities for my mind to ponder as I felt my way along by sliding my feet the way a blind person might if they were negotiating this path without a cane. After several minutes of feeling my way in near darkness, the path came back close to the river. Hearing the sound

I Will Save You to Make You a Blessing

of rushing water far below without being able to see how close it was did little to reassure me. As I came very close to the sound of the river, I encountered a large mudslide completely covering the path. I wondered if the two or three weeks that had expired since the flood would make the mud firm enough to walk on. I couldn't tell if the mud was just a few inches thick or several feet deep. The sound of the river right beside me told me I had better try to make it across, rather than around this one.

After taking several spongy steps, the mud gave way and down I went, both legs disappearing, leaving me up to my thighs in mud and all alone in the darkness. For a moment a feeling of panic and despair came crashing in all around me. I felt buried from the waist down with mud and engulfed in a sense of despair from the waist up. I was totally alone. Not a single human being had a clue where I was. There was no one to call out to, and if I did call out for help, would I alert some wild animal of my helplessness? In the blackness of the night my soul cried out to a God who has promised to be a very present help in times of trouble. It was at this moment that I heard the voice of God. In the stillness of that black night, God's Spirit said, "You are not alone, I have sent heavenly angels to walk by your side." The most amazing peace swept over me. I could genuinely feel the presence of heavenly beings around me.

I tried to move from the grasp of this giant suction cup that held me fast. After a few tries, I was able to rock a little from side to side. I rolled over onto my stomach to allow my leg the freedom to lift from the deep mud holding it fast. With the sound of a suction cup letting go, my leg came free. I instantly knew I now had a new problem. My leg was resting safely up on top of the mud but my foot was minus my slip-on dress shoe. I had no idea how much farther I had to go, but it seemed like it would be an impossibility to continue as I tried to picture myself in stocking feet traversing pressing on in the kind of terrain I had just been over. I knew I had to somehow retrieve the missing shoe from its place of lodging in the deep hole beside me.

Back down into the mudhole went my foot in search of the missing shoe. The mud was stiff enough that it had not collapsed into my shoe, so I was easily able to slip my foot back into the elusive shoe below me. I rolled my toes into a ball in the front of my shoe, creating as tight a fit as possible. I wiggled my foot side to side with this new, inner grip of balled up toes, to try to loosen the shoe, then slowly lifted it up and out of the muddy grave that had been holding it captive. After repeating the process, I was able to slowly lift my other foot with shoe coming up and out to freedom.

Lying on my stomach, I began to crawl to the faint outline of some thick trees and bushes just a few feet away. Reaching the trees that seemed to form a wall at the edge of the path, I was able to stand on solid ground again. I crawled through a narrow thicket to the sound of rushing water far below. I could just make out a narrow footpath on this side of the trees that seemed to be about fifteen to eighteen inches wide, with only a black abyss on the other side that must have rushing water somewhere far below. Apparently others had used this little shelf-like path as sort of a detour around the mudslide. In the deepening darkness this alternative route did not seem all that comforting. The trees and bushes were like a wall on my right side, and the other side simply dropped off straight down to the river perhaps fifty or sixty feet below. I knew that no one would ever find me or know what happened to me if I slipped from this narrow ledge.

In the darkness I inched my way along with the sound of a rushing river far below me as a constant reminder that there would be no second chances. I was so thankful for my unseen guide from heaven who kept me up on that narrow ledge until the path widened and moved safely away from the river's edge. Feeling my way along, I wondered how much farther it could possibly be. After groping my way along for several more minutes, I spotted a flicker of light. At just the moment I was wondering which way to go, someone had come outside and turned on a little flashlight.

As fast as I could, I stumbled my way up the hill to the light that had become a beacon in the night to one very lost and lonely traveler. As I approached the man with the flashlight, I could see a large refugee camp all around him.

"Please sir, can you tell me how much farther it is to Bijia Norte?" I asked.

"Oh, about forty-five minutes," he said.

"Sir, is there any way you could sell me your flashlight?" I pleaded.

I Will Save You to Make You a Blessing

He looked at what must have been a pretty pathetic looking figure standing before him. He asked if I knew the way to Bijia Norte.

"No," I replied.

He said, "I will take you then," and he led the way with a young boy following along. I had forgotten how precious a little beam of light could be, but I would never forget from that moment on. As we walked around more mudslides and deep washes in the pathway, I tried to imagine what it would have been like to find the rest of my way in the darkness.

I asked my kind guide if the young boy was his son. "No," he replied. "He is an orphan from the war that took place recently all through these mountains."

I remembered hearing some of the terrible stories of the war between the Sandanistas and the Contras. This pathway that we were walking on was right through the heart of the territory of many fierce battles. That terrible war left an untold number of little boys and girls without fathers and brothers. This kind man had informally adopted the young boy, giving him a home to grow up in until it was washed away in the flood.

At last, the lantern in front of the building I was staying in came into view. The little shelter had seemed so crude to me at first, but the vivid memories of my experiences that evening made it look like a safe haven now. I knew this kind man was also one that the Lord had intended to bless with some of Lesa's love offering. I gladly gave him a gift to help him in his time of need.

In order to properly appreciate this story, I must share the conclusion that I did not learn myself until several days later. When we finished our work in these mountains we were transported back to the ADRA regional headquarters in Ocatal, then to a hotel to rest for a night before returning to Managua the next day.

As I finished my breakfast at the hotel café the next morning, I spotted another visitor walking across the hotel compound. As we exchanged greetings and shared our business in Nicaragua, I learned he was working as an instructor-trainer with a team of dogs trained to sniff for land mines. "Nicaragua," he said, "is literally dotted with mines that have never been retrieved since the war."

Several tragic accidents had recently taken place since the storm.

Our God is a Very Present Help in Time of Need

Many of these terrible land mines had been dislodged in mudslides, causing them to slide from mountainsides down in and around villages. Just a couple of days earlier, we heard of two children who found a mysterious box in the mud close to their house. They had been blown to pieces while examining this curious object. Just outside of town a cow had also taken a wrong step, ending its life. These recent developments confirmed what he was telling me.

He looked directly at me with some words of caution for my remaining time in Nicaragua. "Whatever you do," he said, "stay away from the Coco River and the surrounding region. It is extremely dangerous."

"Just a few nights ago," I replied, "I was lost without a light for several miles all along the Coco River traversing around and through a constant barrage of mudslides."

He stared at me for a moment or two, then said in a quiet voice, "There are 186,246 land mines unaccounted for, most of them in the area where you were lost." He added, "The smallest of these land mines are designed to remove a man's legs to the waist, and the largest will discharge enough shrapnel to kill an entire company and any thing else in its path for a quarter mile in any direction." He finished by saying, "You are one lucky man to be alive." Then he turned and walked away.

At that moment, standing in the hotel compound, I heard a kind and loving voice say, "I spared your life." I rode in silence in the back of one of the ADRA jeeps all the way back to Managua with a very special awareness that a kind and loving God was surrounding me with His presence. As I finish writing this page of my life's story, I bow my head again to thank my kind and loving Heavenly Father for another opportunity to live and for another day to praise His name. Lucky? Not a chance! I am so thankful that He saved me to be a blessing. Wouldn't you like to take this moment to surrender your life to the One who has spared your life for an eternity? Let's pause for a moment to give Him our all one more time.

18

Conclusion

As I was nearing the conclusion of these pages, I began to ask God, "What do You want me to entitle this book? Lord, I am praying that all who read this book will be able to see a new picture of You on each page of my life's experience. Lord, may it be clear to all that these experiences have everything to do with You and Your amazing faithfulness and nothing to do with me. Lord, what kind of title would You have me give these pages?"

The next morning as I was praying about a new aspect of ministry, my Bible just sort of fell open to the book of Zechariah, chapter eight. My eyes went instantly to a passage I had underlined some time earlier. It was one of those special moments when you hear the voice of God speak to you personally from His word. The last half of verse 13 reads; "I will save you that you may become a blessing. Do not fear; let your hands be strong."

It was such an encouragement and answer to prayers for His leading in our lives and the ministry that He has planned for us. I thanked Him over and over for the personal word of encouragement He had spoken to me that morning as I drove along to work. After some minutes of enjoying the wonders of His presence, He spoke to me again. He said, "I want you to use the words in Zechariah that I spoke to you this morning as the title of the book you are writing." He then repeated in a sweet, gentle voice, "I will save you that you may become a blessing." My eyes became moist as I thought once again of the many times He has saved me, including several not included in the pages of this book. "Lord," I prayed, "I invite

Conclusion

You to use each day of my life to be used as a blessing for You and Your kingdom."

I wonder if you would like to join me in this commitment. Isn't it time for all who have taken the name of our Savior as a Christian to be our utmost for Him in the conclusion of the war for souls on planet Earth? As the eyes of the Lord run to and fro throughout the earth seeking those who are willing to be made a blessing, perhaps you have heard His personal invitation to be one of those special blessings. When He asks, "Whom shall I send, and who will go for us," will you say, "Here am I, send me?"

Has God saved you? Have you been forgiven a multitude of sins? Has Jesus offered to cover your dark record with the merits of His shed blood? If He has, He wants to make *you* **a blessing.**

I would like to close with a special invitation to all who have been "saved to become a blessing." Would you join me in a challenge from God's Word?

"How blessed is the man whose strength is in You. In whose heart are the highways to Zion" (Psalms 84:5 NASB). The "Captain of the Lord of Hosts" is offering a special blessing to all who find their strength in Him. If you are willing to find your strength in Jesus, He is offering to change your heart so completely that your life will be a superhighway leading straight to the kingdom of heaven. I long for that kind of re-creation, don't you? Right now you might feel like there is some needed construction that must first take place before others can travel safely at high speeds to the kingdom of heaven on your highway. I am so glad for the promise that says, if we keep our eyes on Jesus and find our strength in Him, He will have no difficulty bringing to completion the work that He has begun in us. With your full cooperation the necessary construction can be completed rapidly, allowing your highway to be open for travel.

Living in a world that seems to be adding new highways leading to eternal destruction every day, how needful are heavenly highways leading lost and weary travelers to an eternal home where every tear will be wiped away from their eyes. How needful are highways that lead to a heavenly Zion where there will be no more death, no longer any mourning, or crying, or pain. If every Christian would become a superhighway leading to heavenly Zion, how easy it would be for those

I Will Save You to Make You a Blessing

traveling the paths of life to discover the Way, the Truth, and the Life! Wouldn't you like to become one of these special highways? I invite you to take a moment just now, joining me in this special "Highway to Zion" commitment.

> Heavenly Father, I _____ commit my life to You this day, inviting the Holy Spirit to cleanse, instruct, and empower me to be a useful and effective means whereby lost and weary travelers find an eternal home in heavenly Zion.
>
> When the last weary traveler passes through the gate of pearl to their new eternal home in heavenly Zion we will make our way before the throne of grace to behold and worship the Lamb who has taken away the sin of the world. Each of us will be surrounded by those enjoying eternity because we invited our Heavenly Father to make us a useful means for others to find their way to this climactic moment. In concert we will remove our crowns placing them at the feet of Jesus singing, "Worthy, worthy, worthy is the Lamb that was slain to receive power, honor and glory."

Please don't wait long in the forever that follows to personally introduce me to the ones who are standing and singing with you. I am anxious to meet each one.

I pray that as you have taken this journey with me through some of the pages of my life, you too have heard God personally say to you, "I will save you that you may become a blessing."

**For Further Information
the Author may be contacted by:
Phone:** ~~(920) 623-4813~~ (608) 429-4922
**or
e-mail: budds@wi.net**

Made in the USA